Table of Content :

1	**LIFE STAR REFERENCE TABLE**	7
2	**INTRODUCTION**	12
3	**YOUR XUAN KONG LIFE STAR**	23
	Basic Attributes	24
4	**YOUR FENG SHUI ESSENTIALS**	27
	Directions	29
	Taking the Direction using a Compass	33
	Favorable Directions	39
	Unfavorable Directions	49
	Bed Alignment Direction	58
	Best Floor	60
	Personal Grand Duke Direction	65
	Personal Clash Direction	71
	Flying Star Effects	76
5	**THE FIVE ELEMENT**	97

6	**CHARACTERISTICS OF STAR**	109
	The Good	111
	The Bad	117
7	**CAREER AND WEALTH**	123
	Characteristics at work	124
	Suitable Job Roles	128
	Career and Wealth Guide	132
8	**RELATIONSHIPS**	139
	Guide for Relationships	140
9	**HEALTH**	145
	Guide for Health	146
10	**COMPATIBILITY with OTHER LIFE STARS**	151

LIFE STAR REFERENCE TABLE

Year Pillar and Gua Number Reference Table for 1912 - 2055

Animal	Year of Birth			Gua Number for Male	Gua Number for Female	Year of Birth			Gua Number for Male	Gua Number for Female
Rat	1912	壬子 Ren Zi	Water Rat	7	8	1936	丙子 Bing Zi	Fire Rat	1	5
Ox	1913	癸丑 Gui Chou	Water Ox	6	9	1937	丁丑 Ding Chou	Fire Ox	9	6
Tiger	1914	甲寅 Jia Yin	Wood Tiger	5	1	1938	戊寅 Wu Yin	Earth Tiger	8	7
Rabbit	1915	乙卯 Yi Mao	Wood Rabbit	4	2	1939	己卯 Ji Mao	Earth Rabbit	7	8
Dragon	1916	丙辰 Bing Chen	Fire Dragon	3	3	1940	庚辰 Geng Chen	Metal Dragon	6	9
Snake	1917	丁巳 Ding Si	Fire Snake	2	4	1941	辛巳 Xin Si	Metal Snake	5	1
Horse	1918	戊午 Wu Wu	Earth Horse	1	5	1942	壬午 Ren Wu	Water Horse	4	2
Goat	1919	己未 Ji Wei	Earth Goat	9	6	1943	癸未 Gui Wei	Water Goat	3	3
Monkey	1920	庚申 Geng Shen	Metal Monkey	8	7	1944	甲申 Jia Shen	Wood Monkey	2	4
Rooster	1921	辛酉 Xin You	Metal Rooster	7	8	1945	乙酉 Yi You	Wood Rooster	1	5
Dog	1922	壬戌 Ren Xu	Water Dog	6	9	1946	丙戌 Bing Xu	Fire Dog	9	6
Pig	1923	癸亥 Gui Hai	Water Pig	5	1	1947	丁亥 Ding Hai	Fire Pig	8	7
Rat	1924	甲子 Jia Zi	Wood Rat	4	2	1948	戊子 Wu Zi	Earth Rat	7	8
Ox	1925	乙丑 Yi Chou	Wood Ox	3	3	1949	己丑 Ji Chou	Earth Ox	6	9
Tiger	1926	丙寅 Bing Yin	Fire Tiger	2	4	1950	庚寅 Geng Yin	Metal Tiger	5	1
Rabbit	1927	丁卯 Ding Mao	Fire Rabbit	1	5	1951	辛卯 Xin Mao	Metal Rabbit	4	2
Dragon	1928	戊辰 Wu Chen	Earth Dragon	9	6	1952	壬辰 Ren Chen	Water Dragon	3	3
Snake	1929	己巳 Ji Si	Earth Snake	8	7	1953	癸巳 Gui Si	Water Snake	2	4
Horse	1930	庚午 Geng Wu	Metal Horse	7	8	1954	甲午 Jia Wu	Wood Horse	1	5
Goat	1931	辛未 Xin Wei	Metal Goat	6	9	1955	乙未 Yi Wei	Wood Goat	9	6
Monkey	1932	壬申 Ren Shen	Water Monkey	5	1	1956	丙申 Bing Shen	Fire Monkey	8	7
Rooster	1933	癸酉 Gui You	Water Rooster	4	2	1957	丁酉 Ding You	Fire Rooster	7	8
Dog	1934	甲戌 Jia Xu	Wood Dog	3	3	1958	戊戌 Wu Xu	Earth Dog	6	9
Pig	1935	乙亥 Yi Hai	Wood Pig	2	4	1959	己亥 Ji Hai	Earth Pig	5	1

- Please note that the date for the Chinese Solar Year starts on Feb 4. This means that if you were born in Feb 2 of 2002, you belong to the previous year 2001.

Year Pillar and Gua Number Reference Table for 1912 - 2055

Animal	Year of Birth			Gua Number for Male	Gua Number for Female	Year of Birth			Gua Number for Male	Gua Number for Female
Rat	1960	庚子 Geng Zi	Metal Rat	4	2	1984	甲子 Jia Zi	Wood Rat	7	8
Ox	1961	辛丑 Xin Chou	Metal Ox	3	3	1985	乙丑 Yi Chou	Wood Ox	6	9
Tiger	1962	壬寅 Ren Yin	Water Tiger	2	4	1986	丙寅 Bing Yin	Fire Tiger	5	1
Rabbit	1963	癸卯 Gui Mao	Water Rabbit	1	5	1987	丁卯 Ding Mao	Fire Rabbit	4	2
Dragon	1964	甲辰 Jia Chen	Wood Dragon	9	6	1988	戊辰 Wu Chen	Earth Dragon	3	3
Snake	1965	乙巳 Yi Si	Wood Snake	8	7	1989	己巳 Ji Si	Earth Snake	2	4
Horse	1966	丙午 Bing Wu	Fire Horse	7	8	1990	庚午 Geng Wu	Metal Horse	1	5
Goat	1967	丁未 Ding Wei	Fire Goat	6	9	1991	辛未 Xin Wei	Metal Goat	9	6
Monkey	1968	戊申 Wu Shen	Earth Monkey	5	1	1992	壬申 Ren Shen	Water Monkey	8	7
Rooster	1969	己酉 Ji You	Earth Rooster	4	2	1993	癸酉 Gui You	Water Rooster	7	8
Dog	1970	庚戌 Geng Xu	Metal Dog	3	3	1994	甲戌 Jia Xu	Wood Dog	6	9
Pig	1971	辛亥 Xin Hai	Metal Pig	2	4	1995	乙亥 Yi Hai	Wood Pig	5	1
Rat	1972	壬子 Ren Zi	Water Rat	1	5	1996	丙子 Bing Zi	Fire Rat	4	2
Ox	1973	癸丑 Gui Chou	Water Ox	9	6	1997	丁丑 Ding Chou	Fire Ox	3	3
Tiger	1974	甲寅 Jia Yin	Wood Tiger	8	7	1998	戊寅 Wu Yin	Earth Tiger	2	4
Rabbit	1975	乙卯 Yi Mao	Wood Rabbit	7	8	1999	己卯 Ji Mao	Earth Rabbit	1	5
Dragon	1976	丙辰 Bing Chen	Fire Dragon	6	9	2000	庚辰 Geng Chen	Metal Dragon	9	6
Snake	1977	丁巳 Ding Si	Fire Snake	5	1	2001	辛巳 Xin Si	Metal Snake	8	7
Horse	1978	戊午 Wu Wu	Earth Horse	4	2	2002	壬午 Ren Wu	Water Horse	7	8
Goat	1979	己未 Ji Wei	Earth Goat	3	3	2003	癸未 Gui Wei	Water Goat	6	9
Monkey	1980	庚申 Geng Shen	Metal Monkey	2	4	2004	甲申 Jia Shen	Wood Monkey	5	1
Rooster	1981	辛酉 Xin You	Metal Rooster	1	5	2005	乙酉 Yi You	Wood Rooster	4	2
Dog	1982	壬戌 Ren Xu	Water Dog	9	6	2006	丙戌 Bing Xu	Fire Dog	3	3
Pig	1983	癸亥 Gui Hai	Water Pig	8	7	2007	丁亥 Ding Hai	Fire Pig	2	4

- Please note that the date for the Chinese Solar Year starts on Feb 4. This means that if you were born in Feb 2 of 2002, you belong to the previous year 2001.

Year Pillar and Gua Number Reference Table for 1912 - 2055

Animal	Year of Birth			Gua Number for Male	Gua Number for Female	Year of Birth			Gua Number for Male	Gua Number for Female
Rat	2008	戊子 Wu Zi	Earth Rat	1	5	2032	壬子 Ren Zi	Water Rat	4	2
Ox	2009	己丑 Ji Chou	Earth Ox	9	6	2033	癸丑 Gui Chou	Water Ox	3	3
Tiger	2010	庚寅 Geng Yin	Metal Tiger	8	7	2034	甲寅 Jia Yin	Wood Tiger	2	4
Rabbit	2011	辛卯 Xin Mao	Metal Rabbit	7	8	2035	乙卯 Yi Mao	Wood Rabbit	1	5
Dragon	2012	壬辰 Ren Chen	Water Dragon	6	9	2036	丙辰 Bing Chen	Fire Dragon	9	6
Snake	2013	癸巳 Gui Si	Water Snake	5	1	2037	丁巳 Ding Si	Fire Snake	8	7
Horse	2014	甲午 Jia Wu	Wood Horse	4	2	2038	戊午 Wu Wu	Earth Horse	7	8
Goat	2015	乙未 Yi Wei	Wood Goat	3	3	2039	己未 Ji Wei	Earth Goat	6	9
Monkey	2016	丙申 Bing Shen	Fire Monkey	2	4	2040	庚申 Geng Shen	Metal Monkey	5	1
Rooster	2017	丁酉 Ding You	Fire Rooster	1	5	2041	辛酉 Xin You	Metal Rooster	4	2
Dog	2018	戊戌 Wu Xu	Earth Dog	9	6	2042	壬戌 Ren Xu	Water Dog	3	3
Pig	2019	己亥 Ji Hai	Earth Pig	8	7	2043	癸亥 Gui Hai	Water Pig	2	4
Rat	2020	庚子 Geng Zi	Metal Rat	7	8	2044	甲子 Jia Zi	Wood Rat	1	5
Ox	2021	辛丑 Xin Chou	Metal Ox	6	9	2045	乙丑 Yi Chou	Wood Ox	9	6
Tiger	2022	壬寅 Ren Yin	Water Tiger	5	1	2046	丙寅 Bing Yin	Fire Tiger	8	7
Rabbit	2023	癸卯 Gui Mao	Water Rabbit	4	2	2047	丁卯 Ding Mao	Fire Rabbit	7	8
Dragon	2024	甲辰 Jia Chen	Wood Dragon	3	3	2048	戊辰 Wu Chen	Earth Dragon	6	9
Snake	2025	乙巳 Yi Si	Wood Snake	2	4	2049	己巳 Ji Si	Earth Snake	5	1
Horse	2026	丙午 Bing Wu	Fire Horse	1	5	2050	庚午 Geng Wu	Metal Horse	4	2
Goat	2027	丁未 Ding Wei	Fire Goat	9	6	2051	辛未 Xin Wei	Metal Goat	3	3
Monkey	2028	戊申 Wu Shen	Earth Monkey	8	7	2052	壬申 Ren Shen	Water Monkey	2	4
Rooster	2029	己酉 Ji You	Earth Rooster	7	8	2053	癸酉 Gui You	Water Rooster	1	5
Dog	2030	庚戌 Geng Xu	Metal Dog	6	9	2054	甲戌 Jia Xu	Wood Dog	9	6
Pig	2031	辛亥 Xin Hai	Metal Pig	5	1	2055	乙亥 Yi Hai	Wood Pig	8	7

- Please note that the date for the Chinese Solar Year starts on Feb 4. This means that if you were born in Feb 2 of 2002, you belong to the previous year 2001.

To download your Two Black Life Star Reference Chart FREE go to

www.masteryacademy.com/regbook

Here is your unique code for access:

GBSN6012

Introduction

When all is said and done, Feng Shui is the study of how environments affect the people living within them. It can yield advice on which environments, at both a macro and micro level, are 'good' places or 'bad' places to live for given people at given times.

Xuan Kong is only one subsection of the study of Feng Shui and the Life Stars are only one component in the Xuan Kong Feng Shui system. This means that the study of Life Stars gives us only one piece of the overall Feng Shui puzzle but it is an important one!

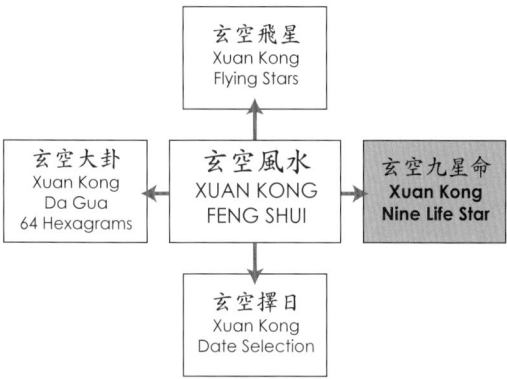

We can use the Xuan Kong Life Star system to help us with a number of practical Feng Shui and interpersonal decisions that make a big impact.
When we assess Feng Shui, we assess four factors:

Environment, Buildings, Time and People. This book has been written to complement a number of other Feng Shui titles;

1. *Feng Shui for Homebuyers – Exterior;*
2. *Feng Shui for Homebuyers – Interior;*
3. *Feng Shui for Apartment Buyers;* and
4. *Pure Feng Shui.*

These other books talk about the influence of Environment, Buildings and Time on Feng Shui. This book looks at the final aspect: **People.**

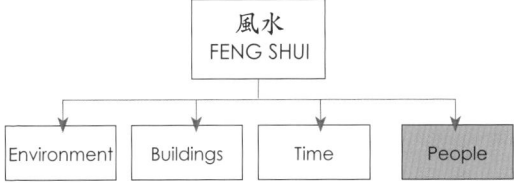

Different people will be affected in different ways by any given environment. The Life Stars directly determine what role the environment plays in the lives of its occupants. Every person is governed by one of the 9 Life Stars. These Stars also help determine key personal characteristics.

In this book, you will learn how the annually changing Xuan Kong Flying Stars interact with your Life Star so that you know what different sectors of your home will bring you. You can then use this information for your own benefit and safety. For maximum benefit, people should seek to align themselves with the direction in their home that yields positive effects. For instance, the #9 Purple Flying Star brings about the potential of career advancement for Star 1 people. Clearly this is a benefit that professionally minded people would like to take advantage of, so they may wish to spend more time absorbing the influence of the #9 Purple Flying Star in their home or place of work. The same Flying Star also indicates a heightened risk of miscarriage for pregnant women though and so pregnant Life Star 1 women should be exercise heightened caution in the presence of this Flying Star, and avoid its influence if possible.

Because the advice generated by this book on Xuan Kong Life Stars takes into account your Life Star when discussing the effects of the Flying Stars, the advice given is highly tailored to your life.

The Positive Side Of You

Your Life Star brings a force to bear on you, wherever you are. This force can have positive or negative effects, depending on the Feng Shui of the environment you reside in.

We are all multi faceted and complex. We have good habits and bad habits; a strong side and a weak side. By correctly tapping into the right Qi your best side will manifest itself more. When you put your best foot forward more in life, more opportunities and success comes your way. Conversely, if you

find yourself under the negative influence of your Life Star, more of your negative personality traits will prevail. Your environment filters out the good or the bad influence of your Life Star. Xuan Kong Feng Shui shows us how we can align ourself to receive the best possible influence. By simply aligning your bed and study desk to correspond with your favourable Personal Directions for example, you can already take one big step towards absorbing the beneficial influence of your Life Star, even whilst you sleep and study! If you are choosing a new home then choosing the correct floor at the correct time will bring further benefits. Avoiding your Personal Grand Duke and Crash Sectors will keep health problems and conflict at bay.

Does all of this mean you must tip-toe around certain rooms in your house or seal them off? No. Feng Shui does not need to become all consuming. If you can easily align your bed so that you receive benefits then why not do so? There are real world limits to what can be done, it is not practical, for instance, to rebuild your home if it does not perfectly cater to the instructions that this book gives. Your ideal floor choice in a condominium may not be available. The list of real world complications goes on.

You can tailor Feng Shui to work for you; making smaller, simple changes so that you reap the maximum possible benefit. The pursuit of good Feng Shui is not intended to take up all of your time and this flexible book is perfect for anyone, no matter how busy or restricted you are in your decisions.

Your Life Star

Everyone falls under the jurisdiction of one of the 9 Life Stars and this will have different consequences for everyone. Your Life Star describes your key skills, characteristics and traits. Some people are creative but reserved, some people are aggressive and driven. What self destructive traits do you have? Do you have a bloated sense of pride or are you prone to gossip? Your Life Star can shine some light on the complexity of your personality and your good and bad traits.

Study of the Life Stars has practical benefits for everyone; it gives you valuable information about others in addition to yourself. Different Life Stars bestow different abilities on people which means that people belonging to each Star will exhibit different characteristics at work. A Star 1 person is diplomatic so they are best suited to roles demanding diplomacy, for example. Accordingly, employers can study the Xuan Kong Life Stars when making work place decisions whilst employees can use the system to help them go about working productively with their colleagues and superiors, even when disagreements arise.

If you become aware of your own harmful tendencies then you can learn to minimize them so you can advance. Similar benefits can be seen in romantic relationships and friendships. Learning that a Star 7 individual needs their space and independence

might help you accommodate this in your dealings with them when you might otherwise have been tempted to be clingy and dependant.

When we understand more about ourselves we can stop ourselves from making mistakes and perhaps forgive certain behaviour in others once we understand where it comes from.

Compatibility Guide

Certain people are, of course, more compatible with each other than others. In partnerships or relationships this takes on a new level of importance. Different Life Stars bestow the qualities of different elements on different people; for example, a Star 1 person has the qualities of water whilst a Star 7 person has the qualities of the Yin Metal element. Just as the elements control, pacify and weaken one another, individuals of the different Stars may dominate, clash with or enrich one another. This book includes a write up of how compatible different Stars are with one another. You may find that a relationship as a Star 1 person with a Star 5 person simply isn't worth the effort. A compatibility guide on each interaction gives you tips on how to best deal with the other Stars for mutual benefit, even taking into account your differences.

Compatible With BaZi Profiling Systems

If you are familiar with the **BaZi Profiling System** then you will be aware that, at first glance, it seems to deal with very similar issues. It can tell us about other preferences and internal view of the world. Do we have an optimistic view of things? Do we blame ourselves too much?

While there is some overlap between the jurisdiction of the Xuan Kong Life Star system and BaZi Profiling System, they are two different systems. They both deal with individual people and their personalities but they are not mutually exclusive. In fact, when studied together, they can be thought of as two pieces of the same puzzle.

The BaZi Profiling System tells us about ourselves and about others. It even tells us things that cannot be observed about others (things people do not communicate). What it can't tell us is how the outside environment plays into the picture. The Xuan Kong Nine Stars help determine *which* qualities are brought out and by what features and external forms in the environment.

Once we know what directions are conducive to good Qi, how external forms (pylons etc) can compound problems related to sectors in the home, which areas of our environment increase the risk of which ailments or even which people can create problems in our lives (compatibility guide) then we can begin shaping our external environment to whatever degree necessary in order to enjoy the most happiness, wealth and success. Xuan

Kong Feng Shui tells you precisely what effect the environment and compass directions will have on which people.

If you are simply interested in learning what makes a person tick rather than making decisions about an ideal environment for them to thrive in then I recommend you take up further study of the BaZi Profiling System. The goal of BaZi is to pinpoint personal deficiencies so that they may be overcome or to highlight personal strengths so that they may be capitalised on.

If you are trying to configure your environment in order to maximize the benefits that your home or place of work bestow upon you in terms of health, wealth and relationships, then the Feng Shui Xuan Kong Life Star system is the one for you.

When you combine the two systems and employ them on yourself you will be able to make the most of your best qualities and then seek out an environment which lets you shine and gives the least resistance. A powerful combination of self improvement and informed decision making!

An Easier Life

Life doesn't have to be difficult. It is possible to effectively dodge conflict, problem situations and health problems if you know they are coming. The Life Stars hold the key to many of the "surprises" that life has in store for us and we can learn to shape our environment to our own advantage. This is exciting stuff! Seeking out the best romantic relationships and business opportunities is a top priority for most people and the power of your Life Star can be called upon in these pursuits.

Even though much is made of the layout of the home with relation to Feng Shui, you won't need to bend over backwards to accommodate the advice given in this book. For instance, where you cannot choose the ideal living floor specified, second and third choices are mentioned. You can take as much or as little from this book as you need without fear of it making you paranoid and prey to "paralysis by analysis". Looking back on your own life, you can most probably think of two or three big mistakes – a bad business deal or choice in romantic partner, perhaps. Avoiding pitfalls of this magnitude in the future is made a whole lot easier when you have some idea of how likely they are to occur. If you can make changes to your environment to further reduce this likelihood then all the better!

I hope that this book expands your world view. Once you know how to utilize them, the Nine Stars can be the harbinger of great fortune instead of misery for you. If you can stay on the 'correct side' of your Star and always position yourself to bask in its positive influence then many happy successes await you.

Joey Yap
July, 2011

 www.facebook.com/joeyyapFB

Author's personal website :
www.joeyyap.com

Academy websites :
www.masteryacademy.com I www.maelearning.com I
www.baziprofiling.com

二黑土星命

Two Black Life Star

Life Star 2	Born in
Male	1926, 1935, 1944, 1953, 1962 1971, 1980, 1989, 1998, 2007
Female	1924, 1933, 1942, 1951, 1960 1969, 1978, 1987, 1996, 2005

- Please note that the date for the Chinese Solar Year starts on Feb 4. This means that if you were born in Feb 2 of 2002, you belong to the previous year 2001.

Your Xuan Kong Life Star

Your Xuan Kong Life Star is Gua #2, and your trigram is called Kun. It looks like this:

For the rest of this book, we will refer to your Gua #2 as **Life Star 2**.

Basic Attributes of Star 2

Your Life Star 2 is of the (Yin) Earth element and as such, it shares some of the traits of Earth. Your Life Star is considered the 'mother' as in mother nature, which serves as the cradle of life. Earth is nurturing, forming the landscape from which life can grow, and this is reflected in your Life Star. You are known for your patient and forgiving nature. You take pleasure in guiding and nurturing others instead of shooting them down, allowing them to grow in the same way the Earth supports life. When the chips are down, you remain a reliable ally, even when others have fled the scene. You are consistent and your stance is wavering. You do not allow yourself to be blown about by every slight breeze. Your gentle and unassuming nature allows other people to confide in you or come to you for help when needed and because of this, you find that many people are willing to rally to your side when necessary.

On the other hand, just like Earth, you may remain fixed and get stuck in one place. There is a danger that you may become complacent or worse, lazy, even about things of great importance. This means that you become comfortable in your current position and may adopt conservative or close-minded views that do not help you grow or improve. Being too patient may result in you taking your own sweet time to think and come to a decision, with the outcome being that you miss out on all that is fast-moving and potentially

Basic Emotions & Temperament

Plus : Trustworthy, sacrificing, diligent, supportive, caring, embracing

Minus: Dependent, suspicious, egotistical, conservative, discriminating

方向

YOUR FENG SHUI ESSENTIALS

The Feng Shui Essentials comprise Feng Shui Directions, the effects of the Xuan Kong Nine Stars in various sectors and areas of your home and workspace, and the Five Elements.

Each of these factors interact with your Life Star in different ways that will affect how your Life Star manifests itself and determine whether or not it brings out good or bad qualities in you.

Directions

Directions

Direction is an integral component of understanding Xuan Kong Nine Life Stars. Different directions in your home and your place of work can either accentuate or depreciate the strength of your Life Star.

Favorable Direction will highlight or enhance the positive traits of your Life Star, while an Unfavorable Direction will diminish or weaken your Life Star and bring out some of its negative attributes.

The Life Star numbers are categorized into two groups: the East Group and the West Group. The names 'East Group' and 'West Group' are just to demarcate the Greater and Lesser Yin transformation of the Tai Ji. They do not literally represent directions.

East Group Life Stars include 1, 3, 4 and 9. Those who are Life Stars 2, 6, 7 and 8 belong to the West Group. The following table will give you a quick reference of the Auspicious and Inauspicious compass directions of the East and West Group.

二黑土星命
Two Black Life Star

East Group 東命

卦 Gua	生氣 Shen Qi Life Generating	天醫 Tian Yi Heavenly Doctor	延年 Yan Nian Longevity	伏位 Fu Wei Stability	禍害 Huo Hai Mishaps	五鬼 Wu Gui Five Ghosts	六煞 Liu Sha Six Killings	絕命 Jue Ming Life Threatening
坎 Kan 1 Water	東南 South East	東 East	南 South	北 North	西 West	東北 North East	西北 North West	西南 South West
震 Zhen 3 Wood	南 South	北 North	東南 South East	東 East	西南 South West	西北 North West	東北 North East	西 West
巽 Xun 4 Wood	北 North	南 South	東 East	東南 South East	西北 North West	西南 South West	西 West	東北 North East
離 Li 9 Fire	東 East	東南 South East	北 North	南 South	東北 North East	西 West	西南 South West	西北 North West

West Group 西命

卦 Gua	生氣 Shen Qi Life Generating	天醫 Tian Yi Heavenly Doctor	延年 Yan Nian Longevity	伏位 Fu Wei Stability	禍害 Huo Hai Mishaps	五鬼 Wu Gui Five Ghosts	六煞 Liu Sha Six Killings	絕命 Jue Ming Life Threatening
坤 Kun 2 Earth	東北 North East	西 West	西北 North West	西南 South West	東 East	東南 South East	南 South	北 North
乾 Qian 6 Metal	西 West	東北 North East	西南 South West	西北 North West	東南 South East	東 East	北 North	南 South
兌 Dui 7 Metal	西北 North West	西南 South West	東北 North East	西 West	北 North	南 South	東南 South East	東 East
艮 Gen 8 Earth	西南 South West	西北 North West	西 West	東北 North East	南 South	北 North	東 East	東南 South East

The concepts of Favorable and Unfavorable are derived from the Eight Wandering Stars system of the Ba Zhai Eight Mansion Feng Shui 八宅風水.

Each of the 8 directions is governed by a Star. These Wandering Stars will affect each Xuan Kong Life Star in different ways. Each Life Star has four Favorable Directions governed by Auspicious Stars: Sheng Qi 生氣 (Life Generating), Tian Yi 天醫 (Heavenly Doctor), Yan Nian 延年 (Longevity), and Fu Wei 伏位 (Stability).

The four Unfavorable Directions are governed by Inauspicious Stars and include Huo Hai 禍害 (Mishaps), Wu Gui 五鬼 (Five Ghost), Liu Sha 六煞 (Six Killings) and Jue Ming 絕命 (Life Diminishing).

The following diagram shows you the Favorable and Unfavorable Directions for Star 2.

Taking the Direction using a Compass

You will need a compass – or alternatively, the Joey Yap iLuoPan app for iPhone available at the Apple App Store – to determine the direction of your Main Door, Bed and Stove. Hold your compass or iLuoPan at waist level as shown on the illustration below. Your compass or iLuoPan will align to the magnetic North on its own. All you need to know is how to take your direction as indicated on the following pages.

Facing Direction of the Main Door

1. Stand about one foot outside the door looking outwards.

2. Use the square base of your compass to help you align yourself parallel to the door.

3. Read the facing direction on your compass.

Facing Direction of the Bed

1. Measure from the head of the bed where your head is placed when you lie down (the direction the headboard faces) and not the direction your feet face.

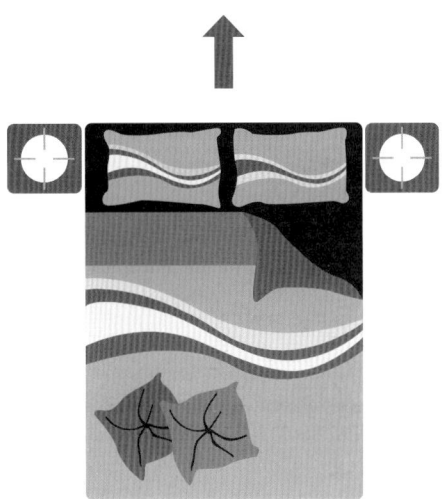

Facing Direction of the Stove

1. For modern (gas or electric) stoves, look at the where direction of the cooking knobs (fire igniters) are pointing to determine its facing direction.

2. For traditional stoves that require wood and fire to work, look for their 'fire mouth' as the facing direction.

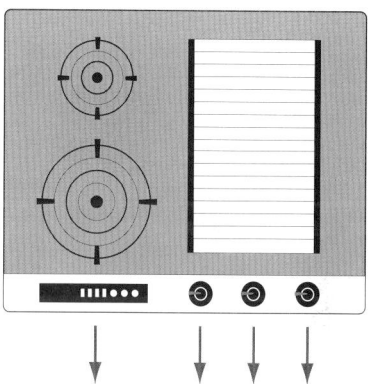

Favorable Directions

Northeast
東北 (37.6°-52.5°)

Life Generating
生氣 (Sheng Qi)

The basic characteristics of the Sheng Qi Star:

It brings about promotions, career advancements, strong money and wealth luck, potential political power and authority, and all-round success.

The Sheng Qi Star represents life-generating Qi or energy. It also represents the Wood Element, and hence, governs the facets of success, authority, nobility, status and wealth in life. Wood relates to growth and advancement in life, and as such is an extremely auspicious Star to tap into. For you, the Northeast direction taps into the Sheng Qi potential.

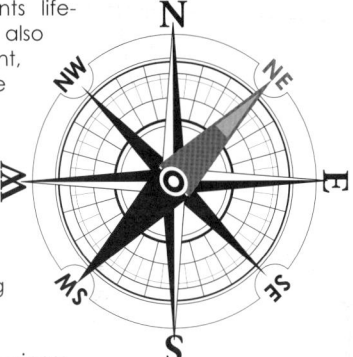

This Star is suitable for business (commercial), career and wealth-related pursuits. It would therefore be ideal for a business or residence to have its Main Door situated in the Sheng Qi sector as it allows you to tap into these energies to create opportunities for profit and long term wealth opportunities.

Sheng Qi is an active star by nature and thus, it is not conducive for rest or sleep-related activities. It is best to avoid having the bed or bedroom located in this sector or for anyone to sleep facing this direction. Use this sector for your work or for active pursuits instead of relaxing ones.

If this sector is missing from a house or is lacking in the office or the premises of a business, the wealth-related aspects of your career or venture will be considerably weakened and it will be a difficult struggle to amass wealth and prosperity.

West
西 (262.6°-277.5°)

Heavenly Doctor
天醫 (Tian Yi)

The basic characteristics of the Tian Yi Star:

It brings about general good luck and well-being, as well as positive mentor luck or the presence of sound advisors and guidance.

This Star represents the Earth Element and is therefore the determinant of noble people (mentors) and people of caliber and status. It also denotes your health prospects and physical wellbeing. As such, the Tian Yi Star is best utilized to help generate guidance for your career or for any project which you've embarked upon. It will bring about the help and assistance of others.

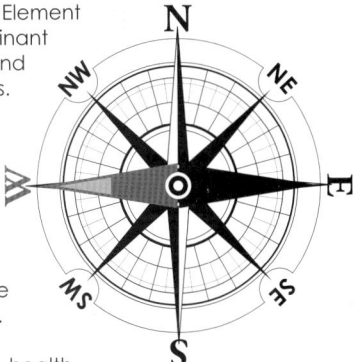

It is also a useful Star for health purposes, and its benefits can be employed when you need to recuperate, recover, or heal from an illness, surgical procedure or health issue.

When the Tian Yin sector is missing from a home or office, your health is likely to suffer because of it. In addition, you will also find help from noble people hard to come by, especially in times of need in life and career matters. You will come across more obstacles and obstructions which you must overcome on your own without the external help of others.

Since the Tian Yi Star represents nobility, it also governs your reputation, respectability, and your oratory powers. It thus has influence on your powers of speech and persuasion, and has some bearing on how you are perceived by others and how well they respond to your verbal overtures.

Northwest
西北 (307.6°-322.5°)

Longevity
延年 (Yan Nian)

The basic characteristics of the Yan Nian Star:

It prolongs and enhances life and improves the quality of your life. It promotes good communication with others which in turn makes for good relationships.

The Yan Nian Star represents the Metal Element, and as such governs speech and the effectiveness of your words. If you are looking to establish good relationships and rapport with others, you will need the help of this Star, since it governs aspects of successful networking, communication and relationship building.

The Yan Nian Star is important for family harmony and domestic bliss. It is also necessary if you wish to build good relationships with co-workers and colleagues. Essentially, it paves the way for smooth interpersonal relations, seldom plagued by misunderstanding, arguments and flare-ups. As such, the presence of the Yan Nian Star is useful for maintaining harmony.

If you are employed in public relations or marketing and you must interact with clients and customers as part of your daily routine, you will find the Qi brought about by this Star very useful to your career.

Do note that if the Yan Nian sector is missing, harmony and unity will be adversely affected, and relations are likely to be tense or strained. At the very least, you can expect more argument and discord with others.

Southwest
西南 (217.6°-232.5°)

Stability
伏位 (Fu Wei)

The basic characteristics of the Fu Wei Star:

It is a Star that promotes calm and keeps you grounded. It allows for peace of mind and rationality. It also promotes good luck.

The Fu Wei Star represents the Wood Element. When qualities or virtues such as calmness and tranquility are required, this is the Star you need! It promotes peace of mind and heightens clarity of thought, so this is also the Star to use if you need to focus, study or make important decisions.

If you wish to practice mediation or undertake religious and spiritual observances, the Fu Wei Star will provide the energies needed for calm and serenity, enhancing mental health and wellbeing.

This Star is most suitably applied to libraries, study areas/zones or other places where concentration is necessary. When considering the home or workplace, this Star can help create areas where the mind can be easily quietened and people can reflect and turn inward.

When the Fu Wei sector is missing from a place, peace of mind will be difficult to attain.

Unfavorable Directions

East
東 (82.6°-97.5°)

Mishaps
禍害 (Huo Hai)

The basic characteristics of the Huo Hai Star:

It denotes potential calamities, accidents, and mishaps. It undermines good efforts and brings about the risk of mistakes and errors.

The Huo Hai Star represents the Earth Element and is the harbinger of mishaps, loss of wealth, sudden (unfortunate) changes or hassles as well as work-related obstacles. What it does is undermine your efforts and bring about sudden obstructions or problems that will result in a loss of time and energy.

If, for example, the Main Door of a property is located in this direction, you can reasonably expect to encounter quite a few obstacles and problems in your daily life. It is best to work around this area particularly if your main door or office is located in the West sector.

The detrimental effects of a negative star are compounded when it is located within an area that is already affected by negative Feng Shui, so pay attention to the negative structures outside this area.

Southeast
東南 (127.6°-142.5°)

Five Ghosts
五鬼 (Wu Gui)

The basic characteristics of the Wu Gui Star:

It brings about betrayal and treachery through back-stabbing, gossip, and rumors. It also denotes endless bickering and fraught tension brought about by arguments.

The Wu Gui Star represents the Fire Element and is the bringer of betrayal, ill-intentioned gossip, rumours, backstabbing, cruelty, petty people and even subterfuge and sabotage. It generally denotes a sense of unease brought upon by less-than-honest speech.

The presence of Wu Gui in a house causes disloyalty and discord amongst family members, affecting relationships and marriages. If it is present in your work place, then you should also watch out for fights and arguments between your colleagues or subordinates and friction or tension with your superiors.

Negative external forms such as (sharp) pylons and jagged rooftops pointing towards a house further aggravate the effects of this Star.

South
南 (172.6°-187.5°)

Six Killings
六煞 (Liu Sha)

The basic characteristics of the Liu Sha Star:

This Star brings about injuries and accidents. It also denotes the possibility of betrayals and dishonesty, and the risk of potential scandals.

The Liu Sha Star relates to the element of Water and is the harbinger of lawsuits and potential scandals. Legal problems at the workplace or adulterous affairs in relation to your marriage or personal relationships could be brought to light.

This Star is also the harbinger of bodily injury, harm and conditions requiring people to undergo physical surgery. Robberies and theft are also likely, and you will have to be careful about what information you share with others and with the general safety of your personal documents and possessions.

Be mindful of the presence of negative external forms, which will compound the adverse effects of this Star. For instance, a Y-shaped road at the Liu Sha sector will result in scandalous affairs, while negative structures as mentioned earlier will compound and exacerbate the harmful effects of the Liu Sha Star.

North
北 (352.6°-7.5°)

Life Threatening
絕命 (Jue Ming)

The basic characteristics of the Jue Ming Star:

It brings about the risk of accidents and major illness, and the threat of miscarriage for pregnant women. It also signals potential for great calamity.

This Star represents the Metal Element and it signifies accidents and illnesses. The energies of the Jue Ming Star are quite severe and so are its adverse effects, bringing with it considerable risk.

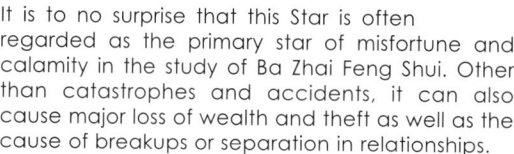

In severe cases, the Jue Ming Star can even cause fatal accidents, ailments or injuries when there are negative external forms outside of the North sector.

It is to no surprise that this Star is often regarded as the primary star of misfortune and calamity in the study of Ba Zhai Feng Shui. Other than catastrophes and accidents, it can also cause major loss of wealth and theft as well as the cause of breakups or separation in relationships.

Bed Alignment Direction

One of the key Feng Shui factors of the bedroom is how your bed is placed. For starters, your bed should preferably be pushed against a wall, with the headboard also against it. The most important thing you can do when laying out your bedroom with regards to Feng Shui is to make sure your headboard is aligned with your Favorable Direction.

Facing Direction, in the case of bed alignment, refers to the direction of your headboard. This means it is the direction your head faces when you lie down on the bed, and **not** the direction that your feet face.

As a Star 2, your Bed Alignment Directions are:

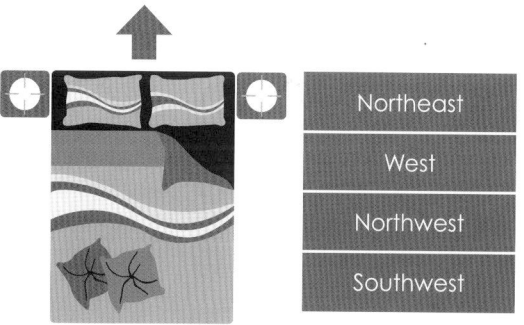

Northeast

West

Northwest

Southwest

Best Floor

A reality of modern life is that most of us do not live in houses these days, instead living in multi story apartments and condominium blocks.

Some of us are pretty mobile and live a nomad-like lifestyle that may require us to stay in high-rise buildings for certain periods of time. As such, it becomes important to select the right floor to reside in. The objective of this is to achieve elemental affinity between you (the occupant) with the energies of a particular floor.

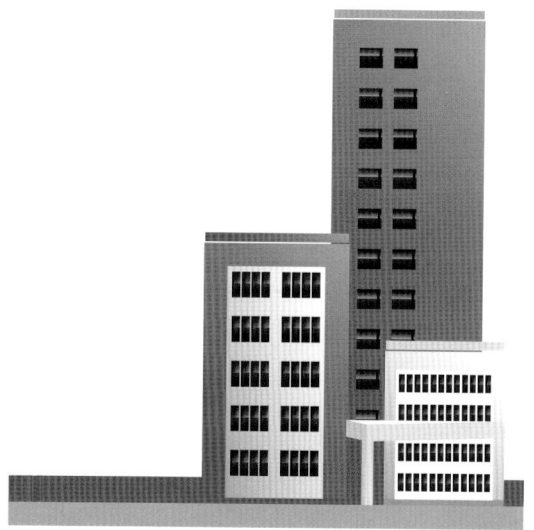

As you are a Star 2 person of the Earth element, the chart below gives you the best floors for you to live on in terms of first choice, second choice, and third choice.

First Choice	Second Choice	Third Choice
5th Floor	2nd Floor	1st Floor
10th Floor	7th Floor	6th Floor
15th Floor	12th Floor	11th Floor
20th Floor	17th Floor	16th Floor
25th Floor	22th Floor	21th Floor
30th Floor	27th Floor	26th Floor
35th Floor	32th Floor	31th Floor
40th Floor	37th Floor	36th Floor
45th Floor	42th Floor	41st Floor
50th Floor	47th Floor	46th Floor

Select :
Fire shaped buildings
Earth shaped buildings

Avoid :
Wood shaped buildings
& Metal shaped
buildings

Personal Grand Duke Directions

Identifying the Grand Duke Sector is important. Your Personal Grand Duke Sector relates to your birth year. For example, if you are born in the year of the Rat then the Rat is your Personal Grand Duke and we know that the Rat sector is North 2.

We want to avoid the harmful properties of this area and as you are a Star 2 person, you can locate your Personal Grand Duke Sector in the following directions:

Personal Grand Duke Directions for Male

MALE Birth Year	Personal Grand Duke	Direction
1917, 1953, 1989, 2025	巳 Si Snake	東南 3 Southeast 3
1926, 1962, 1998, 2034	寅 Yin Tiger	東北 3 Northeast 3
1935, 1971, 2007, 2043	亥 Hai Pig	西北 3 Northwest 3
1944, 1980, 2016, 2052	申 Shen Monkey	西南 3 Southwest 3

Personal Grand Duke Directions for Female

FEMALE Birth Year	Personal Grand Duke	Direction
1915, 1951, 1987, 2023	卯 Mao Rabbit	東 2 East 2
1924, 1960, 1996, 2032	子 Zi Rat	北 2 North 2
1933, 1969, 2005, 2041	酉 You Rooster	西 2 West 2
1942, 1978, 2014, 2050	午 Wu Horse	南 2 South 2

Ideally, you should not have a bathroom or toilet located in these areas of your home above and Sha Qi external features such as pylons, T-junctions, Dead Tree should be avoided. The Sha Qi in the Personal Grand Duke Sector is extremely strong and so all efforts to avoid spending a lot of time in it should be made. It goes without saying that the Personal Grand Duke Sector of your home is not the ideal spot for a bedroom! The Sha Qi in this area of the home is so strong in fact that it is difficult for any further negative Qi to enter!

Personal Clash Directions

Your home will contain Personal Clash Sectors. Spending time in these areas of your home will bring up problems in your life with significant others. As a Star 2 person, you will find your Personal Clash Sectors in the following directions:

Personal Clash Directions for Male

MALE Birth Year	Personal Clash Sector	Direction
1917, 1953, 1989, 2025	亥 Hai Pig	西北 3 Northwest 3
1926, 1962, 1998, 2034	申 Shen Monkey	西南 3 Southwest 3
1935, 1971, 2007, 2043	巳 Si Snake	東南 3 Southeast 3
1944, 1980, 2016, 2052	寅 Yin Tiger	東北 3 Northeast 3

Personal Clash Directions for Female

FEMALE Birth Year	Personal Grand Duke	Direction
1915, 1951, 1987, 2023	酉 You Rooster	西 2 **West 2**
1924, 1960, 1996, 2032	午 Wu Horse	南 2 **South 2**
1933, 1969, 2005, 2041	卯 Mao Rabbit	東 2 **East 2**
1942, 1978, 2014, 2050	子 Zi Rat	北 2 **North 2**

The locations above are a bad place for important features of your home such as the main door, bedroom and kitchen. You should seek to avoid these sectors in the same way you avoid your Personal Grand Duke Sector.

Flying Stars Effects

Each year, the Xuan Kong Flying Stars fly into a different section of a property, be it your residence or your work space. The effects that these Nine Stars have on you will be different depending on your Life Star. In this section you can find out how different Flying Stars in different sectors will effect you with regards to Feng Shui.

The Flying Stars have both negative and positive attributes, but which facets will show when you see a particular Star, depends on the timeliness and the period.

A few of the Nine Stars are inherently negative, a few are inherently positive in nature and some can be both good and bad. Even then, we must remember that the Stars have the capacity to manifest either their positive or negative facets because in Feng Shui, nothing is ever inherently bad or good forever.

When it comes to Flying Stars, it is important to remember this key principle: Forms activate the Stars and the Stars in turn influence the People. This is what you should keep in mind as you read about the effects of the Nine Stars on your Life Star.

1 ★ → 2 Black Life

The effects of the visiting #1 White Star on a 2 Black Life:

In terms of Feng Shui effects, a Star 2 individual who lives or works in an area where the #1 White flies is likely to experience health problems. Star 2 individuals of each gender will be affected in different ways. Men are likely to experience stomach problems and digestive disorders. They may also have to deal with the onset of sex-related issues and troubles, whether in terms of diminished libido or potential complications. Women will also find that they have stomach troubles, but these are likely to come in the form of gastritis. In some cases, it could become chronic and long-term treatment will be necessary. Pregnant women must be aware of the increased risk of complications.

2★ → 2 Black Life

The effects of the visiting #2 Black Star on a 2 Black Life:

In terms of Feng Shui effects, when the #2 Black flies into a particular sector of your home or workspace, it can have a two-sided effect depending on the reaction of the individual in question. On the plus side, #2 Black can bring with it more wealth and possible opportunities that will give you access to more income (both direct and indirect wealth). On the other hand, all this focus on money could cause you to become overly-invested to the point of greed. The Star is the harbinger of health problems for women, bringing wealth but sapping away at health in exchange. Abdominal cramping, stomach issues and pregnancy complications are all made more likely by #2 Black.

3★ → 2 Black Life

The effects of the visiting #3 Jade Star on a 2 Black Life:

In terms of Feng Shui effects, the #3 Jade Star brings about lots of problems; this Star is also known as 'Bullfight Star'. As such, you can expect fights to be fierce and you will find yourself constantly battling opposing opinions and viewpoints from other people. Tension and fractured connections will plague you for as long as the #3 is present, unless you work hard to alleviate the tension and avoid arguments.

In more serious cases, legal disputes and lawsuits could be brought about. In situations where there seem to be no alternatives, the #3 Jade can also cause break-ups and terminations. This could be true even in domestic partnerships and friendships, as well as professional relationships. Furthermore, elderly ladies are likely to suffer from arthritis.

4★ → 2 Black Life

The effects of the visiting #4 Green Star on a 2 Black Life:

In terms of Feng Shui effects, this #4 Green can bring about problems between women and their mothers-in-law if they live in the same house. Arguments will be rife as differences of opinion will not be tolerated, and they are likely to lead to more fighting and tension. You may find yourself suffering from emotional tumult and volatility with the presence of this Star, leading to moments or constant feelings of depression and melancholy. It brings with it the potential for accidents involving animals, and this could mean pets in the home. Furthermore, the presence of the #4 Green denotes hidden tension and agendas, meaning that you might have to deal with someone who has kept something from you for awhile, or come face-to-face with a betrayal or treachery.

5 ★ → 2 Black Life

The effects of the visiting #5 Yellow Star on a 2 Black Life:

In terms of Feng Shui effects, the #5 Yellow brings a dangerous influence with it. Where possible, if you are residing in a sector that has the #5 Yellow for the year, move to another room. If the Main Door is located here, it might be advisable to use the back door for the duration of the year. Furthermore, if you work in this sector, it will also be best to move into another area for the time being. The presence of the #5 Yellow could bring about some serious health implications, including appendicitis and ulcers or serious stomach problems that may require surgery. Cancer is also a possibility.

6★ → 2 Black Life

The effects of the visiting #6 White Star on a 2 Black Life:

In terms of Feng Shui effects, the presence of the #6 White is likely to result in good financial rewards for you. Prosperity is likely, particularly from real estate gains. As such, you will do well to focus on real estate investments and see how you can make your land transactions yield some profits. The energy of this Star will help you gain some much needed secondary income. On the other hand, despite the money you may earn, the Star is likely to make you a bit of a scrooge! This is either a good thing or a bad thing depending on your point of view – saving money you make instead of spending it often pays off in the long run.

7★ → 2 Black Life

The effects of the visiting #7 Red Star on a 2 Black Life:

In terms of Feng Shui effects, the presence of the #7 Red bodes quite well for you. In general, you will enjoy good energy and will find yourself quite lucky in being able to get your tasks completed and your work done. Furthermore, #7 Red brings about good wealth luck for you and you will be exposed to more profit generating opportunities. On the other hand, there is a good chance that you might spend more extravagantly than usual, so you need to keep an eye on your finances and stick to your budget as closely as possible. In terms of personal relationships, if you're married you need to be extra attentive to your marriage as the risk of divorce or separation is increased by the influence of this Star.

8★ → 2 Black Life

The effects of the visiting #8 White Star on a 2 Black Life:

In terms of Feng Shui effects, the presence of the #8 White is good for your financial standing. It brings about auspicious wealth luck, and this is a good opportunity for you to try to get creative with your income and the money that you earn. You could make good progress with attempts at a second income. However, this Star can also bring about a certain solitary asceticism to your life, and you may feel like you want to cut yourself off from the world and act accordingly on your own. This is not necessarily a bad thing, but you will have to be careful as to how far you take it. After all, no one person is meant to be an island unto his or herself!

9★ → 2 Black Life

The effects of the visiting #9 Purple Star on a 2 Black Life:

In terms of Feng Shui effects, the presence of the #9 Purple is beneficial for you if you're female, but not so much if you're male. Indeed, if this Star comes into play at the home or your living space, it will benefit the women much more than the men, and men are liable to feel discomfort living here for long. It is likely to 'chase' men away, but what this means is that men are likely to stay away from the house for longer periods of time. However, this Star brings about the likelihood of romantic affairs and relationships for you. If you're single, this will be a positive development, and you may find yourself fielding a lot of flattering attention! Unfortunately, the #9 Purple can bring about some physical health problems, particularly where your eyes are concerned.

五行

THE FIVE ELEMENTS

The Five Elements

The element of your Life Star 2 is (Yin) Earth, and it is important that you understand the implications of this. In the study of Chinese Metaphysics and Feng Shui, a basic understanding of the Five Elements is integral to success. This section will briefly outline the role of the Five Elements.

The Five Elements are symbolic representations of energy, or Qi. In Feng Shui and in BaZi, the Five Elements are Earth, Metal, Water, Wood, and Fire. The Earth of Star 2 represents the nurturing, pliant earth of the fields. The properties of Earth is that it is flat, representing the vast landscape of the earth itself. Colours associated with Earth are yellow and black.

In order to understand the elements, it's important to understand their relationship to one another. Each element does not exist in isolation. As such, these elements share three important relationships known as 'cycles' that are fundamental to the understanding of Feng Shui: the Productive Cycle, the Controlling Cycle, and the Weakening Cycle.

Productive Cycle

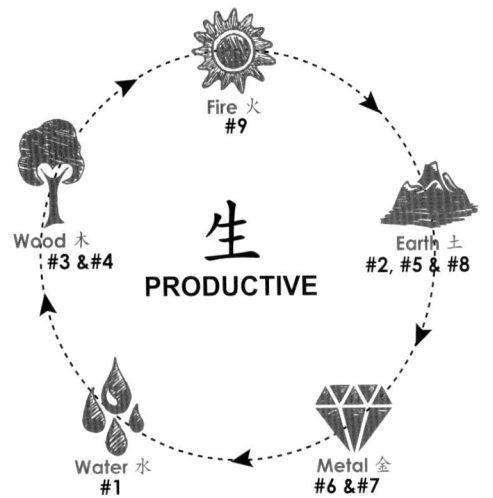

In this cycle,

| Water produces Wood |
| Wood produces Fire |
| Fire produces Earth |
| Earth produces Metal |
| Metal produces Water |

This is a cycle where the elements "produce" one another in terms of providing or helping the growth of another. In the case of Water, then, it produces nourishment for trees and plants (i.e. Wood). An element that produces another element means that it strengthens and grows the element that it produces. Here are some simple metaphors might help you visualize this better:

Water waters soil, producing Wood
Wood makes kindling, producing Fire
Fire makes ashes, producing Earth
Earth is mined, producing Metal
Metal melts, producing Water

Controlling Cycle

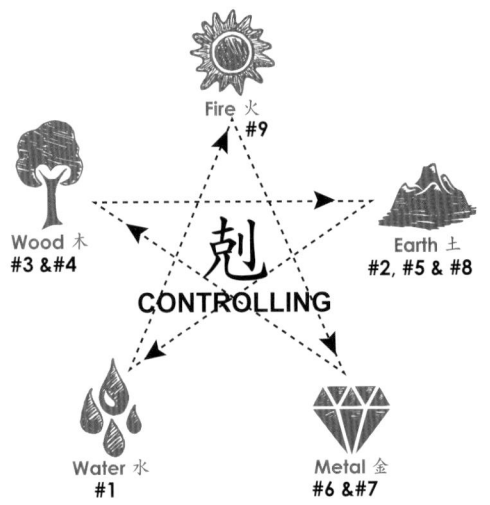

In this cycle,

| Fire controls Metal |
| Metal controls Wood |
| Wood controls Earth |
| Earth controls Water |
| Water controls Fire |

This is a cycle where the elements keep each under in "control": an element is countered or subjugated by its controlling element. In this instance, for example, the element of Water controls Fire by putting it out. Here are some simple metaphors to help you visualize it better:

Water extinguishes Fire
Fire melts Metal
Metal cuts Wood
Wood roots tightly grip Earth
Earth contains Water

Weakening Cycle

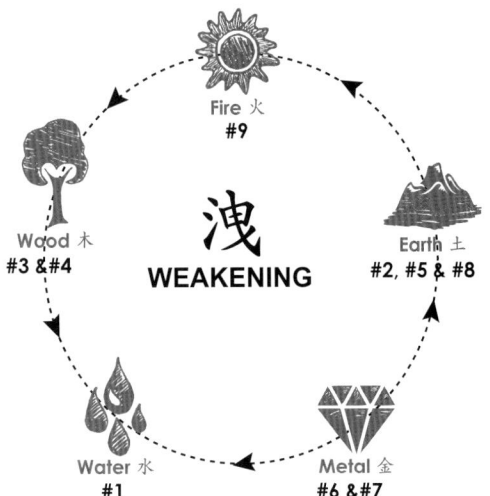

In this cycle,

Water weakens Metal
Metal weakens Earth
Earth weakens Fire
Fire weakens Wood
Wood weakens Water

The Weakening Cycle can be best understood as the reverse of the Productive Cycle, in that the strength of the element is weakened by another in order to keep it in check. Remember, the key to Qi in Feng Shui is balance, and different elements keep other elements from becoming too strong. For example, Wood absorbs Water and therefore weakens it. Again, here are some metaphors for easier visualization:

Water can be partly absorbed by Wood
Wood can be partly burnt by Fire
Fire can be diminished with Earth
Earth is weakened when mined for Metal
Metal is corroded by Water

The following table shows you the Annual Stars for the year 2000 to 2026.

Examine it and figure out where your room lies; in which sector. Take note of the element of that sector and remember that as a Star 2 person, your element is Earth.

2002, 2011, 2020

6 White METAL	2 Black EARTH	4 Green WOOD
5 Yellow EARTH	7 Red METAL	9 Purple FIRE
1 White WATER	3 Jade WOOD	8 White EARTH

2003, 2012, 2021

5 Yellow EARTH	1 White WATER	3 Jade WOOD
4 Green WOOD	6 White METAL	8 White EARTH
9 Purple FIRE	2 Black EARTH	7 Red METAL

2004, 2013, 2022

4 Green WOOD	9 Purple FIRE	2 Black EARTH
3 Jade WOOD	5 Yellow EARTH	7 Red METAL
8 White EARTH	1 White WATER	6 White METAL

2005, 2014, 2023

3 Jade WOOD	8 White EARTH	1 White WATER
2 Black EARTH	4 Green WOOD	6 White METAL
7 Red METAL	9 Purple FIRE	5 Yellow EARTH

2006, 2015, 2024

2 Black EARTH	7 Red METAL	9 Purple FIRE
1 White WATER	3 Jade WOOD	5 Yellow EARTH
6 White METAL	8 White EARTH	4 Green WOOD

2007, 2016, 2025

1 White WATER	6 White METAL	8 White EARTH
9 Purple FIRE	2 Black EARTH	4 Green WOOD
5 Yellow EARTH	7 Red METAL	3 Jade WOOD

2008, 2017, 2026

9 Purple FIRE	5 Yellow EARTH	7 Red METAL
8 White EARTH	1 White WATER	3 Jade WOOD
4 Green WOOD	6 White METAL	2 Black EARTH

2000, 2009, 2018

8 White EARTH	4 Green WOOD	6 White METAL
7 Red METAL	9 Purple FIRE	2 Black EARTH
3 Jade WOOD	5 Yellow EARTH	1 White WATER

2001, 2010, 2019

7 Red METAL	3 Jade WOOD	5 Yellow EARTH
6 White METAL	8 White EARTH	1 White WATER
2 Black EARTH	4 Green WOOD	9 Purple FIRE

These Annual Stars shows you the location of the Stars in a property for the duration of the years specified. Based on the year, the Annual Stars will be located in different sectors of the house. Accordingly, different Annual Stars will affect the Feng Shui of your room in different years.

If the Annual Star of your bedroom is of the same element as your Life Star then the outcome is likely to be prosperous (Productive Cycle). If the Annual Star is your Life Star's controlling element (Controlling Cycle), then the result is likely to be stressful – although this combination is still desirable. But if the Annual Star element is the countering element (Countering Cycle) of your Life Star, then the combination is an unfavorable or inauspicious one for you. (Special note: the #5 Yellow Star is generally an undesirable Annual Star for your bedroom regardless of your Life Star.)

Think about the way the element of the Annual Star and your element (Earth) interact.

Besides the Annual Stars of the year, there also other factors to be considered. These include the Flying Stars chart of your specific house or property with the Sitting and Facing Stars. Advanced students may want to read *Xuan Kong Flying Stars Feng Shui* for further information. These Stars also affect the evaluation of the impact of the Xuan Kong Flying Stars on your property. There are many other ways of assessing the Feng Shui of a property, and it's important to understand that all these factors play an important and related role.

Characteristics of Star 2

We all have our "good days" and "bad days". Feng Shui seeks to help isolate why this happens and provide advice that you can use to make every day a "good day" where you are in your element. This section outlines the good and bad characteristics of your Life Star. In a positive sector of your house or work, the positive attributes of your Life Star will be further enhanced, and you will display more of these characteristics. In a negative sector, the positive attributes will be diminished and the negative attributes will begin to show through. Your bad characteristics will take center stage.

The Good

Nurturing

As a Star 2 person, one of your key characteristics is your ability to nurture others. You are intrinsically good-hearted, and you aim to see the best in everyone. This means that you are also committed to bringing out the best in others. As such, you are always willing to provide guidance and assistance to the people who need it. Others often feel comfortable and secure when relying on you for help.

Diligent

Whenever you embark on a new project, you tend to display a sense of meticulousness and diligence in your work. In this sense, as a Star 2 person, you exhibit the trait of perfectionism. You dislike doing things in a haphazard, disorganized manner. You pay attention to the details and ensure that you oversee every matter so that it is done correctly.

Resourceful

You are able to harness creativity in order to get something done. You're not one to give up easily and concede defeat if something seems hard to do. This is part of your ability to get creative and resourceful in finding solutions to problems that seem insurmountable. What stumps others will rarely stump you, because your mind is already planning the next step in order to find a suitable fix to the problem.

Forgiving

As a rule, Star 2 people are forgiving and magnanimous to a fault. Even if you see the bad in others or have been used or manipulated by folk with dubious ethics, you are willing to give people a second chance to prove themselves. You dislike burning bridges and casting people out of your life. You would rather be kind and afford them the opportunity for redemption and change.

壞

The Bad

Anxious

The downside of taking on the burdens of everyone else is the fact that the Star 2 character is constantly worried about what might go wrong. This is in fact what motivates you to constantly try to fix not only your problems, but the problems of others. You worry quite often about what could go wrong and thus tend to frequently operate from a state of anxiety.

Fussy

As a Star 2 person, you are committed to perfection, but when this tips over to the extreme then you're liable to be someone who is fussy with unrealistic expectations. You may sometimes demand that others perform miracles or achieve the impossible in order to get something done. For this reason, you may become too pernickety and get hung up on the small details, losing sight of the bigger picture.

Submissive

When the Star 2 character is out of balance, it tends to become too yielding and shows no resistance to external forces. As such, you may become too much of a "yes-person" without really standing up for your own beliefs or those of others. Too eager to appease in order to avoid friction or inconvenience, you may fall prey to a certain dependence on others and become overly passive and compliant.

Conservative

When the Star 2 becomes unhealthy, you tend to display characteristics of hardheadedness brought on by an unwillingness to do things differently, or see things differently. You become used to your regular methods and will not make an attempt to go beyond your conservative viewpoint, and will stick to what you're comfortable with. This means that you may conform to an existing system instead of trying to go beyond it.

職業和財富

CAREER AND WEALTH

Characteristics at Work

As a Star 2 person, you may display some of these basic characteristics in professional situations at the workplace and in relation to your career. Being aware of your own key characteristics will help you understand why you act and react to situations, people, and tasks in the way you do.

This section outlines the good and bad characteristics of your Life Star. In a positive sector of your house or work, the positive attributes of your Life Star will be further enhanced, and you will display more of these characteristics. In a negative sector, the positive attributes will be diminished and the negative attributes will begin to show through. Your bad characteristics will take center stage.

• Practical

While you are on the job, you typically tend to focus on what needs to be done. You dislike procrastinating or standing and waiting for inspiration to hit you. Instead, you quickly see what needs to be done and think about practical, realistic ways in which you can do it. This means that you can be relied upon to zero in on a task or problem and sort it out, which makes you invaluable to colleagues, superiors, and subordinates.

• Dedicated

You're not someone who consistently looks for ways to get other people to do your job. Although you can be resourceful and are adept at harnessing people, energy and time in your pursuit to fulfill the requirements of a project, you're ultimately quite a hands-on person who prefers to do things yourself. However, this means that sometimes you bite off more than you can chew in your reluctance to delegate your work.

• Didactic

You're good at teaching and instructing others what to do, possessing the ability to take complex ideas and processes and convey them in a simple, easy-to-understand manner. As such, others tend to learn or benefit from your knowledge when they spend time around you.

• Tactful

As far as your work personality goes, you tend to favor being kind and tactful over being abrasive and confrontational. Your aim is to minimize conflict and prevent other people from feeling attacked, uncomfortable, or unhappy. As such, you're quite careful with your words and will strive to ensure that the other person feels comfortable before you proceed. You possess a natural sense of diplomacy that makes others relax in your company.

Suitable Job Roles

• Manager

This job role suits the Star 2 character perfectly. You are the quintessential manager, because you're the person that others come to when they need to get things organized and operational. You have a sound instincts which make you resourceful and adept at harnessing various disparate forces to your advantage. You are good at telling others what needs to be done and showing them how to do it, although you will have to strive harder to delegate instead of doing everything yourself if you are to succeed in this role.

- ## Real estate, property investment

As someone of the Earth element, you'll do well with things that are constructed on top of it! Star 2 characters will have good skills and instincts when it comes to property management and sales. You will find that you enjoy good wealth luck when you explore these ventures, if it's already something that taps into your interests.

- ## Teachers, educators

You are good at explaining things to others and relaying complex information in a concise and simple way. Because of this, the Star 2 character will also thrive as teachers,

educators, or professors. Your kind and gentle nature will most likely benefit younger children, however, and so working in preschools and nurseries will play further into your strengths.

• Doctors, nurses, healthcare

Because of your generally kind and nurturing nature, you will do well in jobs that require you to care for others and help them heal and get better. Not only do you possess the detail oriented mind needed for the often painstaking and laborious work of medicine and healthcare, you have a strong sense of ethics and commitment that won't allow you to do less than your best.

Career and Wealth Guide

- ## Create consistency

Although you're not someone who enjoys a 9-to-5 desk bound routine, you do prefer consistency and certainty in your job as opposed to a daily roller coaster ride. Having some measure of predictability built into your job allows you to feel more in control and enables you to stop worrying about the "what ifs" in order to focus on the task at hand.

• Speak your mind

Sometimes, your tendency to be supportive can be used to negative ends by others. If you're too compliant or project a submissive attitude to avoid disagreement, others will find it easier to take advantage of you. Furthermore, you'll find it harder and harder to share your real concerns. At the workplace, it is important to learn how to say what you mean and ask for what is rightfully yours – and crucially, to learn to say no when your plate is too full.

- # Learn to delegate

You sometimes want to do everything on your own, which can prove to be a problem when you find it impossible to do everything on your own! You worry too much that others will do things wrong, but taking on too much by yourself can also create extreme amounts of tension and stress for you, particularly as you move closer to a particular deadline or due date.

- ## Cultivate different opinions and perspectives

While you are often gentle-mannered and accepting of others, you can become a little too fond of your own perspective and point of view and resistant towards incorporating new views. This can be a weakness in your career and can also be a problem in terms of amassing more wealth, as you may be reluctant to venture into somewhat risky but potentially profitable avenues, losing out on good opportunities.

• Focus on indirect wealth

You should diversify your options for wealth, as you will do very well if you focus on your ability to garner passive income through side investments, particularly in relation to property. Land-related transactions bode well for you, so don't focus all on earning money only through a stable income. Expand and explore new avenues for extra income.

Famous Personalities :

Jack Welsh, Peter Lynch, George Lucas, Lance Armstrong

人際關係

RELATIONSHIPS

Guide for Relationships

As a Star 2 person, you can be sentimental sometimes in your pursuit of love and relationships. As such, you can enter into hasty or rushed relationships because of your willingness to believe the best in someone else. In general, this is what makes you lovable to others. However, you need to be careful that you don't fall into less-than-ideal relationships because you are too forgiving and too eager to overlook some of the flaws or bad traits that crop up in another person.

You are very nurturing, and this can make the people you're with feel very comforted and safe. You usually tend to want to lesson the pain felt by others and will do anything within your power to try to help them overcome strife or problems. At the same time, you must be careful that your willingness to do everything for others does make them dependent on you. If you're a woman, you may have a tendency to be too "motherly" towards your partner and perhaps even treat them like a child, thus creating room for resentment and suffocation on their part.

Because you care a lot about your partner, it may be hard for you to distinguish your own opinion or thoughts of yourself from those of your partner. You may be too easily influenced by them and willing to believe their judgment of you, and as such surrender some crucial part of your autonomy to them. Although you are capable, resourceful, and resilient, in relationships you may become too submissive and pliant and start to lose your own sense of self. This is something you should guard against.

In matters of love and the heart, you don't really care much for overt displays of affection or sweet talk - these things don't win you over. In fact, you're liable to be quite impatient over these things, as you prefer to be more practical. You show your love in realistic, prosaic ways – like caring for someone when they're sick, as opposed to buying flowers or writing them poetry! At the same time, it can't hurt for you to cultivate the occasional instinct for romance in order to make your partner happy and to give expression to your feelings.

Star 2 in relationships:

You are very trustworthy and serious when it comes to romance, and may display too much kindness.

健康

HEALTH

Guide for Health

Body parts and organs that are related to Star 2: The stomach and the digestive system.

The body parts that are related to Star 2 are the stomach and the organs and processes related to the digestive system, so whenever health issues arise, they are most likely to affect these areas. You are more susceptible than most to stomach ache, piles, constipation, digestive disorders, stomach flu and food poisoning. This is particularly the case if you don't pay attention to your diet and are careless about what you eat. To guard yourself against the problems outlined above, you should be discerning about the things you eat on a regular basis.

Gastritis and issues involving the spleen will also tend to plague you. Star 2 women in particular can suffer from poor blood circulation, and may have trouble or complications when pregnant – so extra care must be taken. Arthritis is something that could set in quite early for Star 2 people, and special attention needs to be given to the joints and the bones from a young age. If something seems amiss or you have concerns about the above, it will be wise to consult your doctor early.

As a Star 2 person you find it hard to simply relax and let go, and in fact one of your most hated activities is sitting around doing nothing! You feel like you must always be doing something useful and are constantly on the move, but this means that you're liable to suffer from stress and worry that contributes to insomnia. This will weaken your immune system and leave you more prone to physical health ailments.

Furthermore, stress will contribute to the likelihood of gastritis and stomach disorders.

Potential health concerns:
Diabetes
Indigestion
Food poisoning
Stress
Sprains & swells
Skin-related diseases

COMPATIBILITY WITH OTHER LIFE STARS

This section examines your compatibility as a Star 2 with other people who have the same and different Stars. No person goes through life completely alone. Relationships with others form the bedrock of good career networking. Friendships and relations with loved ones, spouses, partners and family make everything worth while. It is necessary to understand how compatible people with different Stars are to prevent conflict and missed opportunities. Bear in mind that issues of compatibility are not definite or set in stone. There are exceptions to every rule. In addition, **the quality of Feng Shui** in your environment helps dictate whether positive or negative traits in people manifest themselves and thus it weighs in on the quality of your relationships with those people. This section serves as a good guide on your relationships with other people of different Stars.

As a rule of thumb, Star 2 people are generally quite of a stable, honest and forgiving nature in relationships with others. You are likely to get along with fellow Earth element Star 8. This is because the relationship is likely to be based on mutual interests and affinity, with trust and assistance forming the bedrock of the relationship. Your relationship with Star 5 is

uneasy and they are likely to take advantage of you when at their worst.

Your relationships with people of Stars 3 and 4 will be complicated, as Stars 3 and 4 are of the Wood element and this controls the Earth element. As such, these relationships may not go well in the long run. They may not be ideal for partnerships or friendships as there is a tendency for both parties to hurt each other. Work, communication and efforts to cooperate must be made by both parties for success.

Star 9 proves to be a great help to you as your Noble People. Stars 6 and 7 might start out well for you, but the long term results of such a relationship could end badly. Star 1 people, however, will be particularly good for you in terms of business associations.

The chart below lists element people or sectors you can utilize to improve your compatibility with other Star people.

玄空九星命

XUAN KONG NINE LIFE STAR

	Compatibility with others Stars (Individuals)	Seek help from this element people or use this sector
Star 2	Stars 2, 5 & 8 (Earth Element)	Earth
	Stars 3 & 4 (wood Element)	Fire
	Stars 6 & 7 (Metal Element)	Water
	Star 9 (Fire Element)	Wood
	Star 1 (Water Element)	Metal

Two Black Life Star

巽 SE Xun	離 S Li	坤 SW Kun
4 Green WOOD	**9** Purple FIRE	**2** Black EARTH
3 Jade WOOD	**5** Yellow EARTH	**7** Red METAL
8 White EARTH	**1** White WATER	**6** White METAL
艮 NE Gen	坎 N Kan	乾 NW Qian

震 E Zhen · 兌 W Dui

The following pages will explain in detail the compatibility factor of a Star 2 person with people of all other nine Stars through the Compatibility Meter. The Compatibility Guides give you tips for managing the relationships in question.

| **2** Black | compatibility with | **1** White |

Compatibility Meter

When you and a Star 1 person get together, the outcome is likely to be productive for you, especially from a business point of view. This is largely because the Water element in Star 1 people will loosen, somewhat, and moisten the Earth element in your Star 2. What this means is that you'll find yourself more at ease and less rigid and stubborn in the presence of a Star 1 person. This could work well in a partnership or business venture, as the presence of a Star 1 person might make you more willing to take risks. Ordinarily you tend to let the fast moving opportunities in life pass you by in favor of your comfort zone but a Star 1 person may encourage you, gently, to grab these. You are practically minded and Star 1 individuals are creative which means you can both bring different things to the table; you may be able

to utilize their lateral thinking to help you see things from a new perspective – that is, if you are willing to change the way you do things once in a while!

Compatibility Guide

Although a union between a Star 1 and Star 2 person can be fruitful, you need to be willing to accommodate their different point of view which presents a difficulty for you as once your mind is made up on a matter, it is usually made up for good. Accept that their different point of view can help you expand as a person and encourage growth; it is good to step out of your comfort zone once in a while and this person will make you do so. This person is prone to occasional outbursts and mood swings but if anyone is equipped to handle these it is you, with your forgiving and magnanimous tendencies. Also remember not to let this persons drive "overwrite" your own goals and point of view – you must vocalize your own opinions and objections, which you are not used to doing. It's important to remember where you end and the other person begins, particularly in romantic relationships.

| **2** Black | compatibility with | **2** Black |

Compatibility Meter

When you and a fellow Star 2 person get together, the result is likely to be quite adversarial. This stems from little more than the fact that you are very entrenched in your way of thinking and if you have a different point of view, neither person is likely to budge or try the other persons approach. This proves to be fertile ground for frequent clashes and arguments. You are predisposed to conflict so in terms of a friendship or a relationship it is entirely possible that there will not be any form of attraction. If you are forced together for a work relationship, be prepared for some form of distrust and suspicion. Where teamwork and delegating are involved, this is obviously less than ideal and might make your task of entrusting work even more difficult, leading you to rely more and more on yourself.

Compatibility Guide

It is possible for you to form a good relationship with someone of Star 2 if there is a big gap in age, i.e. one of you is very much older than the other. In this case, the relationship becomes a nurturing one, as the older Star 2 person will be inclined to take care of the other. In an ideal scenario, it will be a relationship of mentorship and genuine guidance. Two Star 2 individuals might therefore get on in a work environment where one person is "learning the ropes" from another or even in some forms of relationship where one more experienced or stable person cares for the other. There are limits to how healthy this can be, however, as the other Star 2 individual can become dependent on your care and guidance, stifling their own autonomy and growth – the exact opposite of your intended consequence!

| **2** Black | compatibility with | **3** Jade |

Compatibility Meter

When you and a Star 3 person get together, there is likely to be quite an interesting outcome. Your interaction is complex and volatile. This is because the Star 3 personality is an aggressive one, and in a healthy relationship or partnership, he or she is capable of spurring you on to achieve your goals. They can inject some excitement into your life and push you towards things at a speed you would not assume on your own. In other words, Star 3 will bring out your sense of ambition and will teach you how to let go of the little things that hold you back. As an anxious person and perfectionist prone to getting hung up on small problems, you need people around you who can reign you in and give you a reality check about the relative proportions and importance of things. In this sense, time spent with a Star 3 person could be very productive for you. On the other hand, Star 3 individuals have some opposing

qualities and they can take advantage of your good nature. Over time these can come to dominate your interactions if you are not careful and this means that entering long term business partnerships with Star 3 people should be done with caution, if at all.

Compatibility Guide

To make this work, you need to be prepared for Star 3's idiosyncrasies. Star 3 people can be quite impatient and jealous, and if they do feel insecure they could bring about your downfall or cause you to fail. You are vulnerable to such an event because you only choose to see the best in others and you forgive easily. In this case, perhaps too easily. This downfall, however, is only likely to come to pass because as a Star 2 person you're unlikely to neglect or give scant attention to the people who matter to you! For a relationship between Star 2 and Star 3 to work, much cooperation and give and take is needed. Keep your guard up without becoming suspicious.

| **2** Black | compatibility with | **4** White |

Compatibility Meter

When you and a Star 4 person get together, the results are complex and hard to predict. This is because you'll find it hard to decide from your perspective or instincts whether or not you're able to get along with a Star 4 person. They are fickle and guarded and you cannot empathize with their seemingly random and haphazard choices. You may well find their personality agreeable but you cannot decipher why they do the things they do and so it might not be best to rely on your own gut feelings alone; if it is a work partnership, for example, you can get the feedback from other associates and colleagues in terms of understanding the Star 4 person, as he or she is likely to flummox you more often than not.

Compatibility Guide

To make this work, there has to be a commitment from both sides. In the long run, a relationship between you and Star 4 will work if it's a serious and formal relationship. In other words, friendships and love relationships are likely to end badly. They are fickle and you are stable so expectations can differ. There is the possibility that work relationships, however, might work out well due to the commitment of both to find common ground, but you must learn to communicate. You will have to bestow a sense of structure and commitment upon the Star 4 individual, which is something you may enjoy doing given your predication towards nurturing others and encouraging their growth.

| **2** Black | compatibility with | **5** Yellow |

Compatibility Meter

When you and a Star 5 person come together, the result is likely to be disharmonious and somewhat tension-filled relationship. Star 5 people are calculative, cunning and controlling. They will seek to govern you and manipulate you and you, being accepting and forgiving, are the perfect prey for this behavior.

Both of you tend to be quite perfunctory and practical in your relations, and both are also quite parsimonious with money matters! In terms of a friendship or relationship, then, this will be a constant source of problems. There will be frequent arguments over who spends money and who has to pick up the bill, and in the long run this can be quite fruitless. Since you forgive most trespasses, Star 5 people may

learn to walk all over you and you may find yourself too accepting of this to stop it. An unhealthy dynamic can evolve quickly.

Compatibility Guide

It will be important for you to tell apart certain Star 5 people who are trustworthy and with integrity, and some who are malicious and with dubious intentions. That's because Star 5 people are likely to fall into extremes. At worst, they can bring scandal and adultery into your life. If you're unable to tell apart the good from the bad, it might be wiser not to forge a connection with them, especially in a love relationship, or even for a work partnership where utmost trust will be important. If you find a Star 5 person abusing your trust then you will have to learn not to forgive and to be less naive. You must stick up for your own interests because they are unlikely to, not always sharing your inbuilt concern for the interests of others.

| **2** Black | compatibility with | **6** White |

Compatibility Meter

When you and a Star 6 person come together, there are likely to be bumps on the road. That is because you are likely to be gracious and warm in your attempt to reach out to the Star 6 person, but the Star 6 person is likely to be somewhat cold and unyielding – at least initially. Star 6 individuals are highly principles being both loyal and just and this can make life lonely for them. To compensate, they set up barriers around themselves which makes them tough to approach. This is particularly true if you're both getting to know each other on a formal and professional basis. It might seem like you're making all the effort in getting things going! You can find their straight talking rude or confrontational and their sense of pride can make them seem undesirable for friendship or romance. They may not always

be highly sociable, instead putting effort into their academic and scholarly interests. This combination of isolation and coldness makes friendships more difficult still.

Compatibility Guide

To make your connection with a Star 6 person work requires some effort, but it's not necessary a bad thing. Relax a little and strive to slowly break down the armor of the Star 6 person through mutual cooperation. Star 6 individuals are a bit of a perfectionist like you, wanting everything done their way because they are afraid to delegate to others, and if you do things that his or her advantage, the Star 6 person will be more than happy to reciprocate. This way, mutual ground can be forged and you'll find that the Star 6 person will appear less guarded and distant. Over time, you can reach them.

| **2** Black | compatibility with | **7** Red |

Compatibility Meter

When you and a Star 7 person come together, things can start out and even continue to go smoothly. Whether or not this is sustainable is debatable and you should proceed with the awareness that things may not be as they initially seem. Star 7 people have the "gift of the gab" and this means they are extremely adept at telling people what they want to hear. They may not necessarily have malicious intentions but you are pure of heart and if they tell you things they think you wish to hear and you believe them then this can create conflict and heartache in the long run. You may also find that you look for different things in life. Luxury and the finer things in life are important to Star 7 individuals. You have no taste for extravagance, being highly practical. In a

relationship, it is easy to see how this can cause problems and lead to dashed expectations.

Compatibility Guide

Your compatibility success will depend quite a bit on the Star 7 character. If it is someone quite flashy and superficial, you will have difficulty trying to merge with them and be on the same wavelength, because you, being practically-minded and focused, give little thrift to such things. It is quite likely that potential chaos and destruction can occur if the Star 7 person is particularly shallow, and you might over invest too much closeness based on something quite trivial and surface-level. Your kindness here can get you hurt in the long run. Hence, you need to proceed with caution and take things slow.

| **2** Black | compatibility with | **8** White |

Compatibility Meter

When you get together with a Star 8 person, the outcome is not set in stone. There is a lot of variety between different Star 8 individuals and their personalities but if you can meet a compatible Star 8 person then you are likely to benefit greatly from them. You are consistent and you give your friendships and relationship everything you can. Star 8 share your principles of honesty and integrity, and as such relationships, friendships, and work partnerships are likely to flower and result in good success for the both of you. Because there is strong mutual attraction between Star 1 and Star 8 people and a basic affinity, conflict and arguments are likely to be short lived and easily put in the past.

Compatibility Guide

As a side note, not all Star 2 and Star 8 individuals are entirely compatible. There are certain Star 8 people who are interested in making a quick buck or quick gains and moving on, and you'll have to be careful not to be ensnared by them. Your kind and trusting nature, coupled with your willingness to give a lot of yourself and be supportive, means that you could easily fall prey to less-honest characters. Keep your guard up and trust even the slightest misgiving until you know for sure what kind of Star 8 personality you're dealing with.

| **2** Black | compatibility with | **9** Purple |

Compatibility Meter

When you and a Star 9 person get together, the result is likely to be warm and comforting. This person will be one of your Noble People and will contribute a lot to your life, particularly in a romantic relationship. You spend a lot of your time caring for and mentoring others. For once, here is someone who will take care of you! In either friendships or relationships with Star 9 individuals, you will feel warm, cared for, and nurtured, and these feelings are likely to grow as become more intimate in the long run. This person plays very well into your need for long term stability and your occasional tendencies to be dependent. This person will be loyal to you as you are loyal to them. Where many other people take advantage of your nurturing and forgiving nature, this person will reward you for it.

Compatibility Guide

While your relationship with this person will be fundamentally good, problems will arise when you start to depend too much on them, or start becoming overly docile and submissive and surrendering to the Star 9 person's every whim and fancy. This is never healthy in any situation. You need to work on your own strength and bring your own personality to the table, or the Star 9 person will become increasingly distant and may draw away from you the more you "merge" yourself with them. In romantic matters, a Star 9 individual is one you will want to keep a hold of. You have a tendency to get carried away in a relationship so you will need to remember to keep some degree of autonomy if you want a healthy, successful relationship.

About Joey Yap

Joey Yap first began learning about Chinese Metaphysics from masters in the field when he was fifteen.

Despite having graduated with a Commerce degree in Accounting, Joey never became an accountant. Instead, he began to give seminars, talks and professional Chinese Metaphysic consultations in Malaysia, Singapore, India, Australia, Canada, England, Germany and the United States, becoming a household name in the field.

By the age of twenty-six, Joey became a self-made millionaire and in 2008, he was listed in The Malaysian Tatler as the Top 300 Most Influential People in Malaysia and Prestige's Top 40 Under 40.

His practical and result-driven take on Feng Shui and BaZi sets him apart from other older, traditional masters and practitioners in the field. He shows people how the ancient teachings can be utilized for tangible REAL world benefits. The success he and his clients enjoy, thanks to his advice, is positive proof that Feng Shui and BaZi Astrology works, whether everyone believes in it or not!

Today, Joey has helped and worked with governments and the wealthiest people in Singapore, Hong Kong, China, Malaysia and Japan. His clients include multinationals, developers, tycoons and royalties. On Bloomberg, he is featured on-air as a regular guest on the subject of Feng Shui annual forecasts. He is retained by twenty-five top Malaysian property developers to help determine suitable candidates to take top management, change their space and Feng Shui mechanism, the way they make decisions, and understand the natural cosmic energies that can influence their decision-making.

Every year he conducts his 'Feng Shui and Astrology' seminar to a crowd of more than 3500 people at the Kuala Lumpur Convention Center. He also takes this annual seminar on a world tour to Frankfurt, San Francisco, New York, Las Vegas, Toronto, Sydney and Singapore.

The Joey Yap Consulting Group is the world's largest and first specialized metaphysics consultation firm. His consultancy, and professional speaking and training engagements with Microsoft, HP, Bloomberg, Citibank, HSBC and many more have seen the benefits of Classical Feng Shui and BaZi find their way into corporate environment and culture. Celebrities, property developers and other large organizations turn to Joey when they need the best.

After years of field-testing and fine-tuning his teachings, he has put together a team in the form of Joey Yap Research International. The objective of this Research Team is to scientifically track and verify the positive impact of Feng Shui and BaZi on subjects and ultimately to assist more people in achieving their life goals.

The Mastery Academy of Chinese Metaphysics which Joey founded teaches thousands of students from all around the world about Classical Feng Shui, Chinese Astrology and Face Reading. Many graduates have gone on to become successful in their own right, becoming sought after consultants, setting up their own consultancy businesses or even becoming educators, passing on Chinese Metaphysics knowledge to others.

Joey has also created the Decision Referential Technology™, offering decision reformation training on how to make better decisions in business and in personal life. He has led his team of highly trained consultants to help clients create more positive change in corporate boardrooms and increase production in their companies, helping people see their business outlook for each year so they may anticipate, plan and execute their strategies successfully.

Joey's work has been featured regularly in various popular global publications and networks like Time, Forbes, the International Herald Tribune and Bloomberg. He has also written columns for The New Straits Times, The Star and The Edge – Malaysia's leading newspapers. He has achieved bestselling author status with over sixty-five books, which have sold more than three million copies to-date.

His success is not limited to matters of Feng Shui and BaZi. Although his success is a product of them, he is also a successful entrepreneur, leading his own companies and property investment portfolio. When not teaching metaphysics or consulting around the world, Joey is a Naruto-fan, avid snowboarder and is crazy for fruits de mer.

Author's personal website :

 www.joeyyap.com

Joey Yap on Facebook:

 www.facebook.com/JoeyYapFB

www.masteryacademy.com | +603 - 2284 8080

MASTERY ACADEMY
OF CHINESE METAPHYSICS
Your **Preferred** Choice to the Art & Science of Classical Chinese Metaphysics Studies

Bringing **innovative** techniques
and **creative** teaching methods
to an ancient study.

Mastery Academy of Chinese Metaphysics was established by Joey Yap to play the role of disseminating this Eastern knowledge to the modern world with the belief that this valuable knowledge should be accessible to anyone, anywhere.

Its goal is to enrich people's lives through accurate, professional teaching and practice of Chinese Metaphysics knowledge globally. It is the first academic institution of its kind in the world to adopt the tradition of Western institutions of higher learning - where students are encourage to explore, question and challenge themselves and to respect different fields and branches of study - with the appreciation and respect of classical ideas and applications that have stood the test of time.

The art and science of Chinese Metaphysics studies – be it Feng Shui, BaZi (Astrology), Mian Xiang (Face Reading), ZeRi (Date Selection) or Yi Jing – is no longer a field shrouded with mystery and superstition. In light of new technology, fresher interpretations and innovative methods as well as modern teaching tools like the Internet, interactive learning, e-learning and distance learning, anyone from virtually any corner of the globe, who is keen to master these disciplines can do so with ease and confidence under the guidance and support of the Academy.

It has indeed proven to be a center of educational excellence for thousands of students from over thirty countries across the world; many of whom have moved on to practice classical Chinese Metaphysics professionally in their home countries.

At the Academy, we believe in enriching people's lives by empowering their destinies through the disciplines of Chinese Metaphysics. Learning is not an option - it's a way of life!

MASTERY ACADEMY
OF CHINESE METAPHYSICS™

MALAYSIA
19-3, The Boulevard, Mid Valley City, 59200 Kuala Lumpur, Malaysia
Tel : +603-2284 8080 | Fax : +603-2284 1218
Email   : info@masteryacademy.com
Website : www.masteryacademy.com

Australia, Austria, Canada, China, Croatia, Cyprus, Czech Republic, Denmark, France, Germany, Greece, Hungary, India, Italy, Kazakhstan, Malaysia, Netherlands (Holland), New Zealand, Philippines, Poland, Russian Federation, Singapore, Slovenia, South Africa, Switzerland, Turkey, U.S.A., Ukraine, United Kingdom

www.masteryacademy.com | +603 - 2284 8080

Mastery Academy around the world

www.masteryacademy.com | +603 - 2284 8080

JOEY YAP CONSULTING GROUP

Pioneering Metaphysics - Centric Personal Coaching and Corporate Consulting

The Joey Yap Consulting Group is the world's first specialised metaphysics consultation firm. Founded in 2002 by renown international Feng Shui and BaZi consultant, author and trainer Joey Yap, the Joey Yap Consulting Group is a pioneer in the provision of metaphysics-driven coaching and consultation services for individuals and corporations.

The Group's core consultation practice areas are Feng Shui and BaZi, which are complimented by ancillary services like Date Selection, Face Reading and Yi Jing Divination. The Group's team of highly-trained professional consultants are led by Principal Consultant Joey Yap. The Joey Yap Consulting Group is the firm of choice for corporate captains, entrepreneurs, celebrities and property developers when it comes to Feng Shui and BaZi-related advisory and knowledge.

Across Industries: Our Portfolio of Clients

Our diverse portfolio of both corporate and individual clients from all around the world bears testimony to our experience and capabilities.

Joey Yap Consulting Group is the firm of choice for many of Asia's leading multi-national corporations, listed entities, conglomerates and top-tier property developers when it comes to Feng Shui and corporate BaZi.

Our services also engaged by professionals, prominent business personalities, celebrities, high-profile politicians and people from all walks of life.

JOEY YAP CONSULTING GROUP

Name (Mr./Mrs./Ms.):_____

Contact Details

Tel:_____ Fax:_____

Mobile :_____

E-mail:_____

What Type of Consultation Are You Interested In?
☐ Feng Shui ☐ BaZi ☐ Date Selection ☐ Corporate Events

Please tick if applicable:
☐ Are you a Property Developer looking to engage Joey Yap Consulting Group?

☐ Are you a Property Investor looking for tailor-made packages to suit your investment requirements?

Please attach your name card here.

Thank you for completing this form. Please fax it back to us at:

Malaysia & the rest of the world
Fax : +603-2284 2213   Tel : +603-2284 1213

www.joeyyap.com

Feng Shui Consultations

For Residential Properties
- Initial Land/Property Assessment
- Residential Feng Shui Consultations
- Residential Land Selection
- End-to-End Residential Consultation

For Commercial Properties
- Initial Land/Property Assessment
- Commercial Feng Shui Consultations
- Commercial Land Selection
- End-to-End Commercial Consultation

For Property Developers
- End-to-End Consultation
- Post-Consultation Advisory Services
- Panel Feng Shui Consultant

For Property Investors
- Your Personal Feng Shui Consultant
- Tailor-Made Packages

For Memorial Parks & Burial Sites
- Yin House Feng Shui

BaZi Consultations

Personal Destiny Analysis
- Personal Destiny Analysis for Individuals
- Children's BaZi Analysis
- Family BaZi Analysis

Strategic Analysis for Corporate Organizations
- Corporate BaZi Consultations
- BaZi Analysis for Human Resource Management

Entrepreneurs & Business Owners
- BaZi Analysis for Entrepreneurs

Career Pursuits
- BaZi Career Analysis

Relationships
- Marriage and Compatibility Analysis
- Partnership Analysis

For Everyone
- Annual BaZi Forecast
- Your Personal BaZi Coach

Date Selection Consultations

- **Marriage Date Selection**
- **Caesarean Birth Date Selection**
- **House-Moving Date Selection**
- **Renovation & Groundbreaking Dates**
- **Signing of Contracts**
- **Official Openings**
- **Product Launches**

Corporate Events

Many reputable organizations and instituitions have worked closely with Joey Yap Consulting Group to build a synergistic business relationship by engaging our team of consultants, led by Joey Yap, as speakers at their corporate events.

We tailor our seminars and talks to suit the anticipated or pertinent group of audience. Be it department, subsidiary, your clients or even the entire corporation, we aim to fit your requirements in delivering the intended message(s).

Tel: +603-2284 1213   Email: consultation@joeyyap.com

Chinese Metaphysics Reference Series

The Chinese Metaphysics Reference Series is a collection of reference texts, source material, and educational textbooks to be used as supplementary guides by scholars, students, researchers, teachers and practitioners of Chinese Metaphysics.

These comprehensive and structured books provide fast, easy reference to aid in the study and practice of various Chinese Metaphysics subjects including Feng Shui, BaZi, Yi Jing, Zi Wei, Liu Ren, Ze Ri, Ta Yi, Qi Men and Mian Xiang.

The Chinese Metaphysics Compendium

At over 1,000 pages, the *Chinese Metaphysics Compendium* is a unique one-volume reference book that compiles all the formulas relating to Feng Shui, BaZi (Four Pillars of Destiny), Zi Wei (Purple Star Astrology), Yi Jing (I-Ching), Qi Men (Mystical Doorways), Ze Ri (Date Selection), Mian Xiang (Face Reading) and other sources of Chinese Metaphysics.

It is presented in the form of easy-to-read tables, diagrams and reference charts, all of which are compiled into one handy book. This first-of-its-kind compendium is presented in both English and the original Chinese, so that none of the meanings and contexts of the technical terminologies are lost.

The only essential and comprehensive reference on Chinese Metaphysics, and an absolute must-have for all students, scholars, and practitioners of Chinese Metaphysics.

The Ten Thousand Year Calendar (Pocket Edition) | The Ten Thousand Year Calendar | Dong Gong Date Selection | The Date Selection Compendium | Plum Blossoms Divination Reference Book | San Yuan Dragon Gate Eight Formations Water Method | Xuan Kong Da Gua Ten Thousand Year Calendar

Bazi Hour Pillar Useful Gods - Wood | Bazi Hour Pillar Useful Gods - Fire | Bazi Hour Pillar Useful Gods - Earth | Bazi Hour Pillar Useful Gods - Metal | Bazi Hour Pillar Useful Gods - Water | Xuan Kong Da Gua Structures Reference Book | Xuan Kong Da Gua 64 Gua Transformation Analysis

Bazi and Structural Useful Gods - Wood | Bazi and Structural Useful Gods - Fire | Bazi and Structural Useful Gods - Earth | Bazi and Structural Useful Gods - Metal | Bazi and Structural Useful Gods - Water | Xuan Kong Purple White Script | Earth Study Discern Truth Second Edition

www.masteryacademy.com | +603 - 2284 8080

Joey Yap's BaZi Profiling System

Three Levels of BaZi Profiling (English & Chinese versions)

In BaZi Profiling, there are three levels that reflect three different stages of a person's personal nature and character structure.

Level 1 – The Day Master

The Day Master in a nutshell is the BASIC YOU. The inborn personality. It is your essential character. It answers the basic question "WHO AM I". There are ten basic personality profiles – the TEN Day Masters – each with its unique set of personality traits, likes and dislikes.

Level 2 – The Structure

The Structure is your behavior and attitude – in other words, how you use your personality. It expands on the Day Master (Level 1). The structure reveals your natural tendencies in life – are you more controlling, more of a creator, supporter, thinker or connector? Each of the Ten Day Masters express themselves differently through the FIVE Structures. Why do we do the things we do? Why do we like the things we like? – The answers are in our BaZi STRUCTURE.

Level 3 – The Profile

The Profile reveals your unique abilities and skills, the masks that you consciously and unconsciously "put on" as you approach and navigate the world. Your Profile speaks of your ROLES in life. There are TEN roles – or Ten BaZi Profiles. Everyone plays a different role.

What makes you happy and what does success mean to you is different to somebody else. Your sense of achievement and sense of purpose in life is unique to your Profile. Your Profile will reveal your unique style.

The path of least resistance to your success and wealth can only be accessed once you get into your "flow." Your BaZi Profile reveals how you can get FLOW. It will show you your patterns in work, relationship and social settings. Being AWARE of these patterns is your first step to positive Life Transformation.

www.baziprofiling.com

BaZi Collections

Leading Chinese Astrology Master Trainer Joey Yap makes it easy to learn how to unlock your Destiny through your BaZi with these books. BaZi or Four Pillars of Destiny is an ancient Chinese science which enables individuals to understand their personality, hidden talents and abilities as well as their luck cycle, simply by examining the information contained within their birth data.

Understand and appreciate more about this astoundingly accurate ancient Chinese Metaphysical science with this BaZi Collection.

Feng Shui Collection

Must-Haves for Property Analysis!

For homeowners, those looking to build their own home or even investors who are looking to apply Feng Shui to their homes, these series of books provides valuable information from the classical Feng Shui therioes and applications.

In his trademark straight-to-the-point manner, Joey shares with you the Feng Shui do's and dont's when it comes to finding a property with favorable Feng Shui, which is condusive for home living.

Stories & Lessons on Feng Shui Series

All in all, this series is a delightful chronicle of Joey's articles, thoughts and vast experience - as a professional Feng Shui consultant and instructor - that have been purposely refined, edited and expanded upon to make for a light-hearted, interesting yet educational read. And with Feng Shui, BaZi, Mian Xiang and Yi Jing all thrown into this one dish, there's something for everyone.

www.masteryacademy.com | +603 - 2284 8080

Continue Your Journey with Joey Yap Books in Feng Shui

Pure Feng Shui
Pure Feng Shui is Joey Yap's debut with an international publisher, CICO Books, and is a refreshing and elegant look at the intricacies of Classical Feng Shui – now compiled in a useful manner for modern-day readers. This book is a comprehensive introduction to all the important precepts and techniques of Feng Shui practice.

Your Aquarium Here
This book is the first in Fengshuilogy Series, a series of matter-in-fact and useful Feng Shui books designed for the person who wants to do a fuss-free Feng Shui.

Xuan Kong Flying Stars
This book is an essential introductory book to the subject of Xuan Kong Fei Xing, a well-known and popular system of Feng Shui. Learn 'tricks of the trade' and 'trade secrets' to enhance and maximize Qi in your home or office.

Walking the Dragons
Compiled in one book for the first time from Joey Yap's Feng Shui Mastery Excursion Series, the book highlights China's extensive, vibrant history with astute observations on the Feng Shui of important sites and places. Learn the landform formations of Yin Houses (tombs and burial places), as well as mountains, temples, castles, and villages.

The Art of Date Selection: Personal Date Selection
With the *Art of Date Selection: Personal Date Selection*, learn simple, practical methods you can employ to select not just good dates, but personalized good dates. Whether it's a personal activity such as a marriage or professional endeavor such as launching a business, signing a contract or even acquiring assets, this book will show you how to pick the good dates and tailor them to suit the activity in question, as well as avoid the negative ones too!

www.masteryacademy.com | +603 - 2284 8080

Face Reading Collection

Discover Face Reding (English & Chinese versions)

This is a comprehensive book on all areas of Face Reading, covering some of the most important facial features, including the forehead, mouth, ears and even philtrum above your lips. This book eill help you analyse not just your Destiny but help you achieve your full potential and achieve life fulfillment.

Joey Yap's Art of Face Reading

The Art of Face Reading is Joey Yap's second effort with CICO Books, and takes a lighter, more practical approach to Face Reading. This book does not so much focus on the individual features as it does on reading the entire face. It is about identifying common personality types and characters.

Easy Guide on Face Reading (English & Chinese versions)

The Face Reading Essentials series of books comprises 5 individual books on the key features of the face – Eyes, Eyebrows, Ears, Nose, and Mouth. Each book provides a detailed illustration and a simple yet descriptive explanation on the individual types of the features.

The books are equally useful and effective for beginners, enthusiasts, and the curious. The series is designed to enable people who are new to Face Reading to make the most of first impressions and learn to apply Face Reading skills to understand the personality and character of friends, family, co-workers, and even business associates.

Annual Releases
2011 Annual Outlook & Tong Shu

Chinese Astrology for 2011 | Feng Shui for 2011 | Tong Shu Desktop Calendar 2011 | Professional Tong Shu Diary 2011 | Tong Shu Monthly Planner 2011 | Weekly Tong Shu Diary 2011

www.masteryacademy.com | +603 - 2284 8080

Educational Tools and Software

Xuan Kong Flying Stars Feng Shui Software
The Essential Application for Enthusiasts and Professionals

The Xuan Kong Flying Stars Feng Shui Software will assist you in the practice of Xuan Kong Feng Shui with minimum fuss and maximum effectiveness. Superimpose the Flying Stars charts over your house plans (or those of your clients) to clearly demarcate the 9 Palaces. Use it to help you create fast and sophisticated chart drawings and presentations, as well as to assist professional practitioners in the report-writing process before presenting the final reports for your clients. Students can use it to practice their Xuan Kong Feng Shui skills and knowledge, and it can even be used by designers and architects!

BaZi Ming Pan Software Version 2.0
Professional Four Pillars Calculator for Destiny Analysis

The BaZi Ming Pan Version 2.0 Professional Four Pillars Calculator for Destiny Analysis is the most technically advanced software of its kind in the world today. It allows even those without any knowledge of BaZi to generate their own BaZi Charts, and provides virtually every detail required to undertake a comprehensive Destiny Analysis.

This Professional Four Pillars Calculator allows you to even undertake a day-to-day analysis of your Destiny. What's more, all BaZi Charts generated by this software are fully printable and configurable! Designed for both enthusiasts and professional practitioners, this state-of-the-art software blends details with simplicity, and is capable of generating 4 different types of BaZi charts: **BaZi Professional Charts, BaZi Annual Analysis Charts, BaZi Pillar Analysis Charts and BaZi Family Relationship Charts.**

Joey Yap Feng Shui Template Set

Directions are the cornerstone of any successful Feng Shui audit or application. The **Joey Yap Feng Shui Template Set** is a set of three templates to simplify the process of taking directions and determining locations and positions, whether it's for a building, a house, or an open area such as a plot of land, all with just a floor plan or area map.

The Set comprises 3 basic templates: The Basic Feng Shui Template, 8 Mansions Feng Shui Template, and the Flying Stars Feng Shui Template.

Mini Feng Shui Compass

The Mini Feng Shui Compass is a self-aligning compass that is not only light at 100gms but also built sturdily to ensure it will be convenient to use anywhere. The rings on the Mini Feng Shui Compass are bi-lingual and incorporate the 24 Mountain Rings that is used in your traditional Luo Pan.

The comprehensive booklet included will guide you in applying the 24 Mountain Directions on your Mini Feng Shui Compass effectively and the 8 Mansions Feng Shui to locate the most auspicious locations within your home, office and surroundings. You can also use the Mini Feng Shui Compass when measuring the direction of your property for the purpose of applying Flying Stars Feng Shui.

Educational Tools and Software

Xuan Kong Vol.1
An Advanced Feng Shui Home Study Course

Learn the Xuan Kong Flying Star Feng Shui system in just 20 lessons! Joey Yap's specialised notes and course work have been written to enable distance learning without compromising on the breadth or quality of the syllabus. Learn at your own pace with the same material students in a live class would use. The most comprehensive distance learning course on Xuan Kong Flying Star Feng Shui in the market. Xuan Kong Flying Star Vol.1 comes complete with a special binder for all your course notes.

Feng Shui for Period 8 - (DVD)

Don't miss the Feng Shui Event of the next 20 years! Catch Joey Yap LIVE and find out just what Period 8 is all about. This DVD boxed set zips you through the fundamentals of Feng Shui and the impact of this important change in the Feng Shui calendar. Joey's entertaining, conversational style walks you through the key changes that Period 8 will bring and how to tap into Wealth Qi and Good Feng Shui for the next 20 years.

Xuan Kong Flying Stars Beginners Workshop - (DVD)

Take a front row seat in Joey Yap's Xuan Kong Flying Stars workshop with this unique LIVE RECORDING of Joey Yap's Xuan Kong Flying Stars Feng Shui workshop, attended by over 500 people. This DVD program provides an effective and quick introduction of Xuan Kong Feng Shui essentials for those who are just starting out in their study of classical Feng Shui. Learn to plot your own Flying Star chart in just 3 hours. Learn 'trade secret' methods, remedies and cures for Flying Stars Feng Shui. This boxed set contains 3 DVDs and 1 workbook with notes and charts for reference.

BaZi Four Pillars of Destiny Beginners Workshop - (DVD)

Ever wondered what Destiny has in store for you? Or curious to know how you can learn more about your personality and inner talents? BaZi or Four Pillars of Destiny is an ancient Chinese science that enables us to understand a person's hidden talent, inner potential, personality, health and wealth luck from just their birth data. This specially compiled DVD set of Joey Yap's BaZi Beginners Workshop provides a thorough and comprehensive introduction to BaZi. Learn how to read your own chart and understand your own luck cycle. This boxed set contains 3 DVDs and 1 workbook with notes and reference charts.

www.masteryacademy.com | +603 - 2284 8080

DVD Series

Joey Yap's Face Reading Revealed DVD Series

Mian Xiang, the Chinese art of Face Reading, is an ancient form of physiognomy and entails the use of the face and facial characteristics to evaluate key aspects of a person's life, luck and destiny. In his Face Reading DVDs series, Joey Yap shows you how the facial features reveal a wealth of information about a person's luck, destiny and personality.

Mian Xiang also tell us the talents, quirks and personality of an individual. Do you know that just by looking at a person's face, you can ascertain his or her health, wealth, relationships and career? Let Joey Yap show you how the 12 Palaces can be utilised to reveal a person's inner talents, characteristics and much more.

Feng Shui for Homebuyers DVD Series

In these DVDs, you will also learn how to identify properties with good Feng Shui features that will help you promote a fulfilling life and achieve your full potential. Discover how to avoid properties with negative Feng Shui that can bring about detrimental effects to your health, wealth and relationships.

Joey will also elaborate on how to fix the various aspects of your home that may have an impact on the Feng Shui of your property and give pointers on how to tap into the positive energies to support your goals.

Discover Feng Shui with Joey Yap: Set of 4 DVDs
Informative and entertaining, classical Feng Shui comes alive in *Discover Feng Shui with Joey Yap!*

You have the questions. Now let Joey personally answer them in this 4-set DVD compilation! Learn how to ensure the viability of your residence or workplace, Feng Shui-wise, without having to convert it into a Chinese antiques' shop. Classical Feng Shui is about harnessing the natural power of your environment to improve quality of life. It's a systematic and subtle metaphysical science.

Walking the Dragons with Joey Yap (The TV Series)

This DVD set features eight episodes, covering various landform Feng Shui analyses and applications from Joey Yap as he and his co-hosts travel through China. It includes case studies of both modern and historical sites with a focus on Yin House (burial places) Feng Shui and the tombs of the Qing Dynasty emperors.

The series was partly filmed on-location in mainland China, and the state of Selangor, Malaysia.

www.masteryacademy.com | +603 - 2284 8080

Home Study Courses

Gain Valuable Knowledge from the Comfort of Your Home

Now, armed with your trusty computer or laptop and Internet access, knowledge of Chinese Metaphysics is just a click away!

3 easy steps to activate your Home Study Course:

Step 1:
Go to the URL as indicated on the Activation Card, and key in your Activation Code

Step 2:
At the Registration page, fill in the details accordingly to enable us to generate your Student Identification (Student ID).

Step 3:
Upon successful registration, you may begin your lessons immediately.

Joey Yap's Feng Shui Mastery HomeStudy Course

Module 1: **Empowering Your Home**
Module 2: **Master Practitioner Program**

Learn how easy it is to harness the power of the environment to promote health, wealth and prosperity in your life. The knowledge and applications of Feng Shui will no more be a mystery but a valuable tool you can master on your own.

Joey Yap's BaZi Mastery HomeStudy Course

Module 1: **Mapping Your Life**
Module 2: **Mastering Your Future**

Discover your path of least resistance to success with insights about your personality and capabilities, and what strengths you can tap on to maximize your potential for success and happiness by mastering BaZi (Chinese Astrology). This course will teach you all the essentials you need to interpret a BaZi chart and more.

Joey Yap's Mian Xiang Mastery HomeStudy Course

Module 1: **Face Reading**
Module 2: **Advanced Face Reading**

A face can reveal so much about a person. Now, you can learn the art and science of Mian Xiang (Chinese Face Reading) to understand a person's character based on his or her facial features with ease and confidence.

www.masteryacademy.com | +603 - 2284 8080

Feng Shui Mastery™
LIVE COURSES (MODULES ONE TO FOUR)

The Feng Shui Mastery™ comprises Feng Shui Mastery Modules 1, 2, 3 and 4. It starts off with a foundation program up to the advanced practitioner level. It is a thorough, comprehensive program that covers important theories from various classical Feng Shui systems including Ba Zhai, San Yuan, San He, and Xuan Kong.

Module One: Beginners Course   **Module Two:** Practitioners Course   **Module Three:** Advanced Practitioners Course   **Module Four:** Master Course

BaZi Mastery™
LIVE COURSES (MODULES ONE TO FOUR)

The BaZi Mastery™ consists of BaZi Mastery Modules 1, 2, 3 and 4. In Modules 1 and 2, students will receive a thorough introduction to BaZi, along with an intensive understanding of BaZi principles and the requisite skills to practice it with accuracy and precision. This will prepare them, and serious Feng Shui practitioners, for a more advanced levels and fine-tune their application skills in Modules 3 and 4.

Module One: Intensive Foundation Course   **Module Two:** Practitioners Course   **Module Three:** Advanced Practitioners Course   **Module Four:** Master Course in BaZi

XUAN KONG MASTERY™
LIVE COURSES (MODULES ONE TO THREE)
*Advanced Courses For Master Practitioners

The Xuan Kong Mastery™ comprises Xuan Kong Mastery Modules 1, 2A, 2B and 3. It is a sophisticated branch of Feng Shui replete with many techniques and formulae, enabling practitioners to evaluate Feng Shui on a more thorough and in-depth basis. The study of Xuan Kong encompasses numerology, symbology and science of the Ba Gua along with the mathematics of time.

Module One: Advanced Foundation Course   **Module Two A:** Advanced Xuan Kong Methodologies   **Module Two B:** Purple White   **Module Three:** Advanced Xuan Kong Da Gua

www.masteryacademy.com | +603 - 2284 8080

Mian Xiang Mastery™
LIVE COURSES (MODULES ONE AND TWO)

The Mian Xiang Mastery™ comprises of Mian Xiang Mastery Modules 1 and 2 to allow students to learn this ancient art in a thorough, detailed manner. Each module has a carefully-developed syllabus that allows students to get acquainted with the fundamentals of Mian Xiang before moving on to the more intricate theories and principles that will enable them to practice Mian Xiang with greater depth and complexity.

Module One:
Basic Face Reading

Module Two:
Practical Face Reading

Yi Jing Mastery™
LIVE COURSES (MODULES ONE AND TWO)

The Yi Jing Mastery™ comprises Modules 1 and 2. Both Modules aim to give casual and serious Yi Jing enthusiasts a serious insight into one of the most important philosophical treatises in ancient Chinese thought. Yi Jing uses sophisticated formulas and calculations to derive the answers to questions we pose. It is a science of divination, and in our classes there is a heavy emphasis on the scientific aspect of it. It bears no religious or superstitious affiliation.

Module One:
Traditional Yi Jing

Module Two:
Plum Blossom Numerology

Ze Ri Mastery™
LIVE COURSES (MODULES ONE AND TWO)

The ZeRi Mastery™ consists of ZeRi Mastery Modules 1 and 2. This program provides students with a thorough introduction to the art of Date Selection both for Personal and Feng Shui purposes. Our ZeRi Mastery™ aims to provide a thorough and comprehensive program on the art of Date Selection, covering everything from Personal and Feng Shui Date Selection to Xuan Kong Da Gua Date Selection.

Module One:
Personal and Feng Shui Date Selection

Module Two:
Xuan Kong Da Gua Date Selection

www.masteryacademy.com | +603 - 2284 8080